A Passion for Victory

Also by Benson Bobrick

The Battle of Nashville

A Passion for Victory

The Story of the Olympics in
Ancient and Early Modern Times

BENSON BOBRICK

ALFRED A. KNOPF

THIS IS A BORZOI BOOK PUBLISHED BY ALFRED A. KNOPF

Text copyright © 2012 by Benson Bobrick
Cover photograph of vase copyright © 2012 by Art Resource
Cover photograph of Jesse Owens copyright © 2012 by Getty Images

For picture credits, please see page 132.

Visit us on the Web! randomhouse.com/kids

Educators and librarians, for a variety of teaching tools, visit us at RHTeachersLibrarians.com

The Library of Congress has cataloged the hardcover edition of this work as follows:
Bobrick, Benson.
A passion for victory : the story of the Olympics in ancient and early modern times / Benson Bobrick. — 1st ed.
p. cm.
"A Borzoi book."
Includes index and bibliographical references.
ISBN 978-0-375-86869-6 (trade) — ISBN 978-0-375-96869-3 (lib. bdg.) — ISBN 978-0-307-97447-1 (ebook)
1. Olympics—Juvenile literature. I. Title.
GV721.5.B63 2012 796.4'8—dc23 2011016036

ISBN 978-0-375-87252-5 (tr. pbk.)

The text of this book is set in 12-point Palatino.

MANUFACTURED IN CHINA

January 2014

10 9 8 7 6 5 4 3 2 1

First Trade Paperback Edition

To Hilary,
volleyball enthusiast

Nothing renders a man more renowned
in his own lifetime than what he can do
with his hands and his feet.

Homer, *The Odyssey*

Losers crept back to their mothers through
dark alleys in embarrassment and shame.

Pindar, *Odes*

The only victory that counts
is the one over yourself.

Jesse Owens

Contents

Chronology

ANTIQUITY

c. 2000 BC—Colonists migrate to an area of Greece later known as Olympia, inland from the Ionian Sea.

c. 1000 BC—An altar to Zeus is established at Olympia.

c. 900–800 BC—A surge in population leads to the spread of independent city-states and a wave of colonization. Greek colonies are established along the coasts of the Aegean, Tyrrhenian, and Black seas and as far away as southern France. Institutions begin to arise designed to unite these scattered communities and reinforce Panhellenic, or all-Greek, heritage. One such institution is the Olympic Games.

776 BC—The first Olympic festival is held at Elis, Greece, to court the goodwill of the gods. It features a single event—a footrace won by a cook from Elis named Coroebus.

c. 750 BC—Olympic-style events are among the highlights of *The Iliad* and *The Odyssey,* composed by Homer at about this time.

570 BC—The first golden age of the Olympic Games begins.

476 BC—At Olympia, the sanctuary to Zeus is expanded into a religious complex that draws devotees

from all over Greece. For the sports competitions, a big new stadium is also built.

229 BC—Rome begins its conquest of Greece.

146 BC—Greek resistance to Roman rule is mercilessly crushed.

144 BC—The first Olympic Games under Roman auspices are held.

80 BC—The sanctuary at Olympia is sacked during the first of several Roman civil wars.

27 BC—Caesar Augustus, the first Roman emperor, proclaims a peace throughout his empire and inaugurates a new, prosperous age for the Mediterranean world. For the next three hundred years, the Olympic Games thrive.

AD 312—Constantine the Great proclaims Christianity the official religion of the Roman Empire. The Games decline.

AD 394—All pagan festivals are banned by Emperor Theodosius I. The Olympics are officially condemned.

AD 426—At the command of Theodosius II, Olympia (including the Temple of Zeus) is destroyed.

AD 522—The remaining buildings at Olympia are leveled by an earthquake. In subsequent years, floods from nearby rivers bury in silt the whole area where the stadium had stood.

MODERN PERIOD

1612—The Cotswold Olimpick Games are founded in England.

1766—An Oxford scholar discovers the site of the ancient Olympic Games in Olympia, Greece.

1829—French archaeologists unearth part of the original Temple of Zeus.

1850—William Penny Brookes founds the Wenlock Olympian Society at Much Wenlock in Shropshire, England.

June 23, 1894—Baron Pierre de Coubertin convenes the first Olympic Congress at the Sorbonne in Paris, France. The International Olympic Committee is formed.

April 6, 1896—The first modern international Olympic Games open in Athens, Greece.

1900—The second Olympics are held in Paris, France, in conjunction with the Paris World's Fair.

1904—The third Olympics are held in St. Louis, Missouri, in conjunction with the St. Louis World's Fair.

1906—The Intercalated Olympic Games are held in Athens, Greece.

1908—The fourth Olympics are held in conjunction with the Franco-British Exhibition in London, England.

1912—The fifth Olympics are held in Stockholm, Sweden. The Games take hold.

1914–1918—World War I. The sixth Olympics cannot be held due to war but are honored in name.

1920—The seventh Olympics are held in Antwerp, Belgium.

1924—The first Winter Olympics are held at the foot of Mont Blanc in Chamonix, France, as part of the eighth Olympic Festival. The Summer Olympics are held in Paris, France.

1928—The ninth Olympics. The Winter Games are held in St. Moritz, Switzerland. The Summer Games are held in Amsterdam, Netherlands.

1932—The tenth Olympics. The Winter Olympics are held in Lake Placid, New York. The Summer Olympics are held in Los Angeles, California.

1936—The eleventh Olympics. The Winter Games are

held in Garmisch-Partenkirchen in Bavaria, Germany. The Summer Games are held in Berlin, Germany. These were the so-called Nazi Olympics.

1939–1945—World War II. The twelfth and thirteenth Olympics cannot be held due to war but are honored in name.

1948—The fourteenth Olympics. The Winter Games are held in St. Moritz. The Summer Games are held in London. The Paralympics are founded by Ludwig Guttmann.

Prologue

On the night of April 14, 1912, a young American athlete fought for his life in the icy waters of the North Atlantic as over fifteen hundred others around him (including his own father) drowned. His name was Richard Norris Williams, and four days before, he had embarked on the world's largest ocean liner, the *Titanic*, for the United States, where he was bound for Harvard University on a tennis scholarship. The *Titanic*, however, collided with an enormous iceberg, and all his hopes for the future seemed to go down with the ship. Somehow he managed to climb into a collapsible lifeboat and was rescued six hours later with a handful of others after drifting in the sea. But he was in bad shape. He had spent so much time in the freezing water that doctors were sure he would lose both legs. When they asked his permission to amputate, though, he refused. To excel at tennis was his heart's deep dream. Over the next several months, he devoted himself to rehabilitation and exercise and gradually regained his nimbleness and strength.

Williams went on to become a tennis star at Harvard and an American Open and Wimbledon champion, and on July 21, 1924, in Paris, France, he won gold in the tennis mixed doubles at the Olympic Games.

His heroic and inspiring story is but one of many that

Richard Norris Williams practicing at the West Side Tennis Club in 1913, a year after he survived the sinking of the Titanic.

highlight the history of the Olympics. The Games go back thousands—yes, *thousands!*—of years and have a remarkable history as their importance in the world of sport has ebbed and flowed.

Today, the Games are at high tide. They are a global event on a truly majestic scale. Held every two years, with Summer and Winter Games alternating, they are watched by billions of people on TV and generate tremendous revenue. A coveted prize, they are the object of maneuvering by international sports federations, national Olympic committees, and other semi-political groups.

At the same time, the Olympics have become ever more high-tech. In the beginning, runners carried the Olympic torch, the Games' great symbol. Then, in 1956, for example, it was borne partway by planes and pickup trucks. Twenty years later, in 1976, for the twenty-first modern Olympics, held in Canada, a torch was lit by the sun's rays at the Temple of Hera in Olympia, Greece, and carried by runners to Athens, where an ionic sensor converted the flame into electrical impulses that were transmitted to Ottawa, Canada, by satellite. That electrical charge was then converted by a laser beam back into the Olympic flame, which runners carried by torch to Montreal.

This is space-age stuff! But no matter how large or commercial the Games become, it is always the individual stories of personal striving, self-sacrifice, exceptional effort, and, from time to time, good sportsmanship that make the Olympics the stirring and memorable spectacle they are. Who can forget, for example, Fanny Blankers-Koen, the "flying housewife" from Denmark, who was several months pregnant with her third child when, against all odds, she won one gold medal after another in 1948 in track and field? Or fourteen-year-old Nadia Comaneci, a tiny Romanian gymnast, who in 1976 charmed the world with her perky nature and incredible skill? Or the Japanese gymnast Shun Fujimoto, who in the same Games completed his complicated routine on the pommel horse and rings despite having shattered his kneecap in a tumbling run?

They all belong to the long and surprising saga of Olympic sport. This book is the story of how it all began, and how the modern Games came to be.

The Olympic torch at the 2010 Winter Games in Vancouver.

CHAPTER ONE

The Games Begin

Thousands of years ago, sports fans stood in stadiums like our own and cheered like crazy for the athletes they adored. One fan in the second century AD wrote to a friend, "Oh, I can't describe the scene in mere words. You really should experience firsthand the incredible pleasure of standing in that cheering crowd, admiring the athletes' courage and good looks, their amazing physical conditioning—their great skill and irresistible strength—all their bravery and their pride, their unbeatable determination, their unstoppable passion for victory! I know that if you were there in the Stadium, you wouldn't be able to stop applauding."

He was talking about one of the ancient Olympic Games. By then, the Games were an established institution and had been occurring every four years without fail for almost a thousand years. For nearly that long, they had also been the rage of the Mediterranean world.

In addition to the Greeks, many ancient civilizations, including those in Egypt, Crete, and Celtic Ireland, incorporated athletic festivals or contests into their annual cycle of celebrations. But none kept going for as long as the Olympics have. Yet when the Olympics began, who could have imagined they would have such staying power? Their main purpose was to help hold widespread Greek communities together by a shared event.

By the eighth century BC, various Greek peoples had settled along the shores of the Mediterranean and adjacent seas. There were many differences between them, which eventually gave rise to rival city-states, like Athens and Sparta. But they had their "Greekness," or Hellenic nature, in common. So the idea was to have a Panhellenic, or all-Greek, celebration that would affirm their common bond.

Only much later did the Games include representatives from other nationalities, and sportsmen from colonies as far away as Africa and Spain.

Over time, the Games took on a life of their own. They

The stadium at the 2008 Beijing Olympics.

remained communal but acquired the status of tradition. The determination to keep them going would outlast war, famine, turmoil, and even the conquest of Greece itself. They became a symbol of continuity amid the changing fate of nations and revolutions in world affairs.

The track on which footraces were held at the ancient Games in Olympia, Greece.

Today, the Olympic Games are huge multicultural, multimedia events. They are global extravaganzas in which almost every nation takes part. Heroes of the Games enjoy enormous popularity and stature, and the principles the Olympics represent—athletic striving, fair play, goodwill among men—continue to excite the enthusiasm of sports fans throughout the world.

Yet the ancient Olympics could hardly have had a more humble start. As far as anyone knows, the first recorded Olympic event took place in 776 BC, when a two-hundred-yard footrace was held in a meadow beside the Alpheus River in Olympia. The race was won by a man named Coroebus, from the nearby town of Elis, where he worked as a cook. Ideas for a local festival began to take hold, but for a dozen or so years the two-hundred-yard footrace was the only Olympic contest. Then other races were added, drawing larger crowds. New events, too, joined the program, including the discus throw, the chariot race, the long jump, the javelin throw, wrestling, and boxing.

The footraces were of various lengths. The shortest, known as the stade, was a dash the length of the running track or stadium (hence its name), which at Olympia measured two hundred yards. There was also a double stade race (up and down the track) and a two-and-a-quarter-mile run (twenty times around it). As depicted in ancient art, the contestants were anything but lean or spare-looking, like some modern runners, but had substantial upper-body strength and bulging calves and thighs. "They evidently combined," as one historian observes, "a driving knee action with a punching, piston-like movement of the arms to gain extra momentum." Many sprinters, in fact, run like that today.

The footraces were run over a surface of layered sand along a track with as many as twenty lanes. At the starting line, there was a stone slab into which grooves for toeholds were cut. As the runners took their places—in an order determined by lot—they warmed up for a few minutes, then (instead of going into a crouch like modern sprinters) stood up with their arms stretched forward, one foot slightly advanced. The blast of a herald's trumpet sent them off. False starts were checked severely and offenders were struck by an official with his whip. Eventually (in the fourth century BC), the Greeks devised a starting mechanism

A vase from the sixth century BC depicting a footrace.

known as the hysplex, which featured a series of starting gates released by strings.

The last of the race events (introduced in 520 BC) was unlike any other. It was more a military field exercise than a race. Greek foot soldiers known as hoplites lined up and, at a signal, began to toil as best they could two times up and down the track in full body armor weighing about fifty pounds. According to the Greek historian Plutarch, the event was meant to remind the public that the real point of athletic excellence was the development of martial strength and skill.

In those days, there was no record keeping or timing of events, so there were no records to be broken or means to compare achievements from year to year. Each Olympics was a world of competition unto itself.

Some events were much like our own. Others—such as the discus and javelin throws, long jump, boxing, and wrestling—were somewhat different. The discus, for example, weighed about three times as much as a modern discus and, instead of being thrown after a complete rotation, was pitched "from a fixed-feet position . . . with centrifugal force generated by flexing the knees and twisting the trunk."

A Greek statue from the fifth century BC of a discus thrower.

In the long jump, there was a takeoff board, and athletes helped propel themselves forward by swinging metal dumbbells in their hands. These dumbbells weighed from five to ten pounds. Instead of slowing the athletes down, the weights apparently enabled them to make amazing jumps, for the pit was fifty feet long.

From vase paintings, we also know that the javelin was thrown with the help of a loose cord. The cord was looped around two fingers, and after the thrower took a

A third-century BC Greek statue of a boxer with leather thongs tied around his hands resting after a match.

The popular chariot race is depicted on a clay hydria (a large water jug) from the seventh century BC.

few steps forward, he extended his arm and hurled the javelin in an upward arc. The unwinding cord spun the spear like a bullet, enabling it to sail distances of over one hundred yards.

There were two kinds of wrestling: standing and ground (which modern wrestling usually combines). In the first, a combatant circled his opponent and tried to throw him to the ground. A score was made with each throw, and the first to get three throws won. In ground (or mud) wrestling, the opponents tussled in a pit of wet sand until one of them was pinned. Since there were no timed rounds, sheer endurance often determined who won.

Similarly, in ancient boxing there were no rounds, breaks, or even weight divisions. A man had to go the distance once he was in the ring. Instead of padded gloves, boxers wrapped leather thongs tightly around their hands. That made their hands even harder, and with every blow the leather strips would cut into the skin.

These sports were popular, but the biggest and most popular of all was the four-horse chariot race introduced at the Olympics in 680 BC. It eventually replaced the footrace as the kickoff event. The chariot race was held in a rectangular area called the hippodrome, where bareback riding and riding without stirrups also took place. The starting gate of the hippodrome was V-shaped, like the prow of a ship. It had a rope barrier across a row of stalls, and the rope was released by timed stages for an even start. Up to forty chariots might be entered in what was an arduous test of stamina and skill. The chariots were small two-wheelers, open at the back, with four spokes to a wheel. The driver stood exposed, as in a cart. The race went round and round the track for about nine miles, with many hairpin turns. Every turn circled a central post. Almost invariably, it was a violent event with bloody pileups and fatal accidents, which always roused the crowds.

The ancient Greek dramatic poet Sophocles vividly describes such a wreck in *Electra,* one of his plays:

> *At the sound of the bronze trumpet, off they*
> *started, all shouting to their horses and urging*
> *them on with the reins. The clatter of the*
> *rattling chariots filled the whole arena, and the*
> *dust flew up as they sped along in a dense mass,*
> *each driver goading his team unmercifully in*
> *his efforts to draw clear of the rival axles and*
> *panting steeds. . . . Then one team of colts got*
> *out of hand and bolted as they finished the*
> *sixth lap. As they turned into the seventh, they*
> *crashed head-on with another. After that, team*

An illustration from a medieval philosophy book of (from left) Plato, Seneca, and Aristotle.

crashed into team and overset each other. Soon the whole plain was full of wrecks. Yet [one of the charioteers] Orestes got his horses safely past the disordered mass of teams. At each turn of the lap, he reined in his inner trace-horse and gave the outer one its lead. Each time his hub just grazed the post. But at the last turn he erred and struck the post. The hub was smashed across, and he was thrown across and tangled in the reins. As he fell, his horses ran wild across the course. When the crowd saw him fallen, they cried out, "How young he was and gallant!" "How sad his end." When at last the runaway team was stopped, he was so mangled not even his friends could recognize his corpse.

The order of bouts, heats, and lanes for racing was assigned by drawing lots. For the combat events, the contestants gathered in a circle, and a helmet or an urn was passed around. In the urn were matching pairs of marked tokens or chips. Everyone took a token and was paired with whoever drew a match. If there happened to be an odd number of contestants, whoever drew the unmatched token got a free pass to the next round.

In time, there were also combined contests like the pentathlon. This fivefold event involved a footrace, the long jump, the discus throw, the javelin throw, and wrestling. It was meant to highlight all-around skill, and the pentathlete was the most admired of all ancient athletes. The Greek philosopher Aristotle wrote: "Beauty in a young man consists in having a body that is both handsome to look at yet lithe and quick and sturdy enough to hold up under violent blows. That is why pentathletes are the most attractive, being trained for both power and speed. Such men in their prime are good-looking and awe-inspiring at the same time."

A very different combined combat sport called pankration was introduced in 648 BC. Its name essentially means "anything goes." It combined boxing and wrestling and was the fiercest of all events. There were few rules and almost no holds were barred. You could kick, strangle, and even beat your opponent to death if you had to. About the only thing you couldn't do was bite him or gouge out his eyes. The bout went on for as long as it took for someone to win, which happened— short of death—when an opponent was beaten senseless or signaled his surrender by raising the finger of one hand.

Like the chariot race, the pankration drew wild crowds. In keeping with its savage character, it was held before a towering pagan altar compacted out of the calcined ashes and charred remains of sacrificed beasts.

Detail from a Greek vase from the third century BC of the pankration event.

Long before the Olympic Games became a highly organized festival, many of the events had become features at local meets. A good deal about the early character of the Games can be learned, in fact, from the two great epic poems of Homer, *The Iliad* and *The Odyssey*. Both were composed not long after the first little footrace at Olympia took place. The story of *The Iliad* unfolds during the last year of a conflict known as the Trojan War, a semi-legendary struggle (possibly based on an early Greek expedition) between the Trojans and the Greeks. The Trojans were a powerful people who at the time occupied a large city called Troy, which was located in Asia Minor, the site of modern Turkey. The war lasted ten years, and *The Iliad* describes the setbacks experienced by the Greeks when one of their great warriors, Achilles, refuses to fight. At length, however, Achilles agrees to take up arms, and victory over the Trojans is assured. At that point, the Greeks decide to interrupt their assault on the city of Troy to honor a fallen comrade named Patroclus with funeral games.

As in the later Olympics, the chariot race in *The Iliad* is the main event. One of the Greek chieftains, Menelaus, is favored to win, but a young competitor by the name of Antilochus plans to give it a shot. His father, a wise elder named Nestor, tells him he can win if he runs a smart race. Each driver takes his place. Then:

> *They curled their whips above their horses' backs,*
> *Smacked them with the reins, and with hurried yells*
> *Were off, streaking across the plain*
> *Away from the ships, dust rising up under*
> *The horses' chests like a line of thunderheads,*
> *Their manes streaming in the jets of wind.*

The race is close, but thanks to strategy, Antilochus wins.

Afterward, there is a boxing match. Two men step up. One boasts:

> *"Let me tell you this,*
> *And it's a sure thing: Anybody fights me,*

I'll bust him wide open and crush his bones.
Better have his next of kin standing by
To carry him out when I'm through with him."

After they wrap their knuckles in oxhide thongs,

They stepped into the middle with hands held high
And were all over each other with flurries
Of hard punches, snapping jabs to the jaw,
And the sweat was flying from their arms and legs.

Finally, one of them catches the other with an upper-cut, and his friends drag him off

                         with feet trailing,
Spitting out clots of blood, head hanging to one side.

Rembrandt painted this portrait of Homer in 1663.

Not a pretty sight! Next comes a wrestling bout ("where cunning intelligence counts as much as strength"), followed by footraces, mock armed combat, the discus throw, and the javelin throw. All these contests eventually found their way into the Olympic program of events.

Homer's other epic, *The Odyssey,* is about the wide wanderings of Odysseus, another mighty warrior and Greek leader, who at the end of the Trojan War tries to find his way home. In the course of his journey, he is constantly drawn off course and has every kind of adventure. It is an incredibly exciting story. At one point, he stops in the coastal land of the Phaiakians, a Greek-speaking people, who kindly refurbish his ship but then, before he sets sail, invite him to join in their feasting, songs, and games. Once the feasting and musical entertainment are over, one of the Phaiakian leaders exclaims:

> *"Now for the track and field; we shall have trials*
> *in the pentathlon. Let our guest go home*
> *and tell his friends what champions we are*
> *at boxing, wrestling, broadjump and foot racing."*

An expectant crowd gathers, and many young athletes compete.

During a time-out, the host suggests that Odysseus might want to show them what he can do. Unaware of his godlike strength, they think he is a simple sea captain. But the homesick warrior is in no mood for sport:

> *"Why do you young chaps challenge me?*
> *I have more on my mind than track and field."*

One young athlete thinks that's a lame excuse. He suggests that Odysseus doesn't want to compete because

> *"You never learned a sport, and have no skill*
> *in any of the contests of fighting men."*

What an insult! "Odysseus frowned, and eyed him coldly, saying: 'That was uncalled for, friend, you talk like a fool.'" Then, still wrapped in his cloak, he casually picks up the heaviest discus and with one swing sends it spinning out of sight. Turning to the other youths, he asks, "Anyone else?" Speechless, they call it a day.

Chapter Two

Sport in the Ancient World

As such stories tell us, from time immemorial a love of competitive athletics was a significant feature of ancient Greek life. Thanks to the Greeks, it is also a big part of our own culture. It is reflected not only in the modern Olympic Games but, as one writer notes, in our World Cup soccer tournaments, Super Bowls, and tennis opens. From the Greeks, too, we get our preoccupation with youthful bodies and beautiful physiques. Most Greeks "worked out"—even politicians, philosophers, and writers. It is said that the Greek philosopher Plato (probably the greatest philosopher who ever lived) won accolades in wrestling at an important festival of games.

"Nothing renders a man more renowned in his own lifetime," wrote Homer in *The Odyssey,* "than that what he can do by his hands and feet." Then, as now, Olympic victors were more than athletic heroes: they were local and national idols, whom painters and sculptors sought to endow with immortal fame.

Held every four years to coincide with the second full moon after the summer solstice—that is, about mid-August, often in blistering heat—the Games attracted the premier athletes from throughout the Greek world.

A large stadium was built to accommodate fifty thousand spectators, with a judges' stand, a running track, and a horse-racing track, or hippodrome. Next to the stadium was a building complex with locker rooms, steam baths, massage parlors (where the athletes got a rubdown with powder and oil), and other facilities familiar to us today from modern athletic clubs. This was the famous gymnasium, or gym, where the men stripped down for their regular workouts. (*Gymnos* in Greek means "naked," and in the all-male ancient Olympic Games, the contestants competed in the nude.)

There was good reason for the athletes to coat themselves with powder (or dust) and oil. In the blistering sun, the oil helped to keep weathered skin moist (just as suntan lotion does today), while powdered grit enabled

The palaestra in Olympia, as it looked in 2010.

contestants to grip their opponents, whose oiled bodies might otherwise slip away. After a workout, there was a plunge bath, where the athletes could wash themselves off. Sometimes, however, they just scraped themselves clean with an implement called a strigil, which had a curved and channeled blade.

By the stadium there was a courtyard with cubicles arranged around a square sandpit, where practice in hand-to-hand combat (boxing, wrestling, and the like) took place. There was also a palaestra, or wrestling school, with colonnades, changing rooms, a common or social room where the young men relaxed, and a room where punching bags (usually sacks filled with fig seeds and sand) were hung from the ceiling or stored.

Over time, the ancient Olympic Games, with their ever-growing complex of temples, racetracks, arenas, wrestling schools, bathing facilities, colonnades, and civic and religious monuments, covered some sixty acres and occupied the whole of the grassy plain in the Alpheus River valley.

In the gymnasium, the men trained to gain speed, agility, muscle tone, and strength. They also experimented with high-protein diets and abstained from alcohol and sweets. Some lifted big stones and other weights to bulk up.

Then, as now, the Games were attended by coaches, personal trainers, doctors, and paramedics, who prepared splints for fractures, stitched up cuts, and applied herbal and mineral remedies to infected wounds. An extract of willow bark (containing aspirin) was used to treat inflammation. A potent ointment containing zinc oxide, aloe,

A coin from the third century BC with the head of Zeus, the king of the Greek gods.

and opium was applied to sore joints and muscles and used to ease sprains.

Although the athletes at Olympia competed in the nude, nobody knows how or why the custom began. According to one story, it started at the Olympics of 720 BC, when a sprinter won the stade after losing his loincloth during his run. A runner from Sparta (one of the Greek city-states) wondered whether running naked might help with speed. So he shed his own loincloth and just happened to win the double stade event. That created a lot of excitement, and the idea caught on.

In the run-up to the Games, all aspiring athletes took part in lesser tournaments and qualifying trials and had to engage in at least ten months of practice before they were allowed to compete. They also had to swear an oath to Zeus, the king of the gods, that they would work for a final month under the watchful eye of the Olympic judges, who ranked them in order of skill and power and selected the events in which they would compete.

They also had to swear that they would do nothing to disgrace the Games. In case the athletes were tempted not to take the oath seriously, they were made to file past a row of statues that preserved a living likeness of those condemned for bribes. The gist of the inscription on each was "You can only win at Olympia with the speed of your feet and the strength of your body," and they were decorated with a threatening image of Zeus wielding his thunderbolt. The judges in turn swore to be impartial and incorruptible in the verdicts they handed down.

In conclusion, the judges told the athletes, "Only those among you who have worked hard enough to qualify for these contests and have managed, in the process, to rid your lives of everything base may proceed. But those among you who have not trained themselves to this level—let them wander where they please, for they have no business here." All this was made more solemn by religious rites. In a ritual at the start of the Games, a bull or ram was sacrificed and its blood poured onto the earth.

In short, athleticism and ferocity were mingled in about equal measure in the program of the Games. The tenor of the events was also diverse. Boys as well as men were allowed to compete, and in a very limited way, women were, too. Women could enter teams of horses they had trained in the chariot race and were granted a small festival of their own at Olympia every four years with one type of event: footracing on a shortened track. But only maidens (unmarried women) could compete. Married women, in fact—for reasons that remain obscure—were not even allowed to watch the Games and if caught doing so could be put to death. Perhaps it was

The ruins of the sanctuary of Hera, wife of Zeus, in present-day Greece.

A statue of Plato at the modern-day Academy of Athens.

not considered decent for married women to look at unclad men.

Every now and then there were exceptions. A woman named Kallipateira, who belonged to a family of champions, brought her son to the Olympic boys' boxing competition in 404 BC. She expected him to win, and to witness his triumph, she disguised herself as a man. When her son prevailed, she leapt over the fence in joy and inadvertently shed her disguise. According to the rules, she should have been thrown off a cliff. But since she was not only the mother of an Olympic champion but the daughter and sister of Olympic champions, she was spared.

The all-maiden games were called the Heraea, in honor of Hera, wife of Zeus. Unlike the men and boys, the maidens did not compete in the nude but "in short dresses unhitched at one shoulder . . . with their hair flying loose."

In no sense did the Greeks look down on women as athletes. After all, one of the great figures of Greek mythology was a huntress, Atalanta, as fleet of foot as any man. Another myth described an all-female tribe, the Amazons, that could fight as well as an army of men. So there existed in the Greek mind an idealized image of women as supreme in athletics and war. As a practical matter, moreover, some Greeks (the philosopher Plato among them) thought it wise to allow women to acquire military skill. For who would "man" the barricades of a town or city, he asked, if the men were away at war? Such skill required strength, which athletics helped to instill.

Plato's opinion had clout. Even in his own day, he was recognized as a great thinker and had founded the famed

Athenian Academy, the first institution of higher learning in the Western world. Moreover, his remarkable *Dialogues*, a series of philosophical discussions on thirty-six topics, are so beautifully written, logical, and clear that they came to represent the high point of ancient Greek language and thought. His unique method of teaching—by refusing to answer a question without raising another in its turn—had been acquired from his own immortal teacher, Socrates. Plato's given name, by the way, was actually Aristocles. But a wrestling coach playfully dubbed him Plato, meaning "fatso," because he was quite stout. And so the greatest philosopher in the history of the world has come down to us with a nickname of gentle ridicule.

Though the Games drew increasingly large crowds, athletes and spectators alike had to fend for themselves once they arrived. On the whole, the accommodations were dismal. Today, the Olympic Village, where athletes live and gather, is usually a fancy and comfortable affair. But the early Olympic Village resembled a shantytown of tents, dens, and improvised wooden shacks. Most people had to pitch camp in the open fields. "Aren't you scorched there by the fierce heat?" wrote one ancient fan to a friend. "Aren't you crushed in the crowd? Isn't it difficult to freshen yourself up? Doesn't the rain soak you to the skin? Aren't you bothered by the noise, the din, and other such things? Yet you seem to put up with all this gladly when you think of the gripping feats you will see."

Such inconveniences seem not to have discouraged enthusiasts from making the trip. "People from all walks of life," we are told, "made their way to the Games.

Princes and tyrants from Sicily and southern Italy sailed up the river in splendid barges, and ambassadors came from various towns, vying with each other in dress and paraphernalia. The rich came on horseback and in chariots; the poor came on donkeys, in carts, and even on foot. Food sellers came loaded with supplies, for there was no town near Olympia. Merchants flocked in with their wares. Artisans came to make figurines that pilgrims could buy to offer to their gods. Booths and stalls were set up; tents and huts were erected, for only official delegates were given accommodation in the magnificent guest house known as the Leonidaion. Most visitors looked for a suitable spot to put down their belongings and slept each night under the summer skies. The crowds were so large that by sunrise on the first day of the Games, there was probably not a single space left from which to see the events." Eventually, the facilities improved when an expansive colonnaded hostel and banqueting pavilion were built.

But in the early days, before stadium seats were built, spectators sat on the grassy slopes of the hills above the track. Only the twelve Olympic judges sat in seats, which were more like thrones, made of stone. In a single seat opposite them sat the priestess of Demeter, goddess of the harvest, who represented the principle of fertility at the Games.

Though the Olympics were not the only sports festival of note in ancient Greece, they were the most important and were known as the Sacred and Crown Games. In part that was because they were dedicated to Zeus, king of the gods. The other three big sports festivals—known collectively as the Panhellenic Games—were the Pythian

The remains of the starting line at the Delphi Stadium, the site of the Pythian Games.

Games, held every four years near Delphi in honor of the god Apollo; the Nemean Games, held every two years near Nemea (also in honor of Zeus); and the Isthmian Games, held every two years near Corinth in honor of Poseidon, god of the sea. Many Greek city-states and other communities also held their own contests. (In 566 BC, for example, Athens founded the Panathenaic Games.) All these Games took place in a four-year cycle known as the Olympiad—named after the Olympics—which was one of the ways the Greeks measured time. Within a few hundred years, "a calendar of competitive athletic meets was so firmly established in the Greek-speaking world" that a special class of full-time athletes emerged who went from one festival to the next in search of accolades. (These athletes were professionals and not at all like the amateur athletes who would participate in the early Olympics of modern times.)

A statue of King Leonidas in present-day Sparta, Greece, which was the home of the notoriously brutal ancient warriors.

Moreover, to help ensure the success of the Games, a so-called Olympic Truce was established early on throughout the Hellenic world. This truce was a four-month armistice during which no military action could take place.

Its aim was to enable both athletes and spectators to travel safely to and from the Games. The truce did not always hold. In 364 BC, for example, the Games were disrupted by fighting that broke out between the residents of two rival towns. There were also boycotts and other rifts. In 424 BC, the Spartans were banned from competing. In 380 BC, the Athenians walked out. Even so, the idea of the truce created a precedent—embraced in modern times—for harmonious competition between otherwise hostile states.

Yet good sportsmanship was scarcely a hallmark of the Games. Nor did contestants take pride in simply performing well. There were no state or national teams, and no awards for second or third place. Every athlete came to compete as an individual and played to win. The training for the Games was strenuous, and the contests themselves, as we have seen, were often terrific ordeals. The word "athlete" comes from the Greek word *athlos,* meaning "one who suffers for a prize." Similarly, the Greek word for a contest is *agon,* from which we get the word "agony," meaning "extreme pain." Although the Olympics proved even more brutal later under the Romans, the Greeks themselves did not always go in for a clean fight. As early as the seventh century BC, they had to introduce a rule against finger breaking. Even so, it is said, one Sicilian wrestler in the fifth century BC won two bouts in a row by breaking all his opponent's fingers.

It was humiliating enough to be beaten, but unsuccessful athletes were also sometimes mocked and ridiculed. "Losers crept back to their mothers through dark alleys in embarrassment and shame," wrote the Greek poet Pindar. They might even be singled out as pathetic for all time.

This happened to one boxer named Apis, whose opponents set up a mock statue to him "because he never hurt anyone."

Some would rather die than suffer that fate. In 564 BC, a two-time defending Olympic champion in the pankration was on the verge of being strangled to death when he got a good grip on his opponent's foot. With a tremendous final effort, he broke it—just as he himself expired. His opponent, in agony, unaware of his own triumph, raised his finger to signal his own defeat—and the victory went to the dead man.

Timidity, of course, was frowned upon. But sometimes an athlete would simply bow out if he thought he didn't stand a chance. One boxer from Alexandria at the Olympics held in AD 25 "took one look at his opponents and ran away." He was fined for cowardice—an exceptional disgrace. Yet one can easily see how a contestant might be cowed. From time to time, a good fighter, however

The temple of Zeus in Athens, as it stands today.

strong, might find himself matched against an opponent of Herculean size. Since a bout could end in death, to fight seemed like suicide.

On the face of it, it was hardly worth the risk. After all, winners received no material reward. All they could officially hope for was an olive branch cut from a tree in the sacred grove of Zeus. But far more was involved. At the end of each contest the names of the victor, his father, and his city-state were proclaimed by heralds to the crowd. So family and national pride were both at stake. The victor also got to set up a statue to himself in the sacred grove nearby. When winners returned home, moreover, they were paraded like heroes through the streets, entertained at banquets, and even granted an annual salary or stipend for life. Some people even thought them semi-divine. In fact, their very sweat mixed with the dust scraped from their bodies was sometimes bottled as a therapeutic salve.

Not surprisingly, some winners couldn't wait to tell the world what they had done. Scarcely had he humbled all rivals in the two-and-a-quarter-mile race in 328 BC, than a runner named Aegeus ran all the way home to Argos, sixty miles away.

To gain a victory in the chariot race could also be a path to power. To begin with, it took wealth to finance the chariot and its team. So like today, when most people who enter politics are rich, the victor became a social standout and a candidate for the elite. In the late fifth century BC, one wealthy Athenian entered no fewer than seven chariot teams at Olympia, multiplying his chances of gaining the crown. As a result, he took the first, second, and fourth places in the race. His name was Alcibiades, and he went on to enjoy a prominent if controversial career in Greek life.

Seven hundred years later, a Roman athlete turned senator, Marcus Aurelius Asclepiades, emphasized the stellar achievements of his own athletic career. He had been a champion in the pankration, he tells us:

> I was the invincible, immovable, matchless
> victor around the athletic circuit—winning
> every contest that I entered. I was never
> challenged; no one ever dared to challenge me. I
> never ended a contest with a draw nor disputed
> any decision. I never retired from a bout nor
> failed to turn up; I never gained victory thanks
> to imperial favor, nor in any newly concocted
> games, but won my honors in the sandpit
> of every meeting which I entered, correctly
> going through all the preliminary procedures.
> I competed in three lands—Italy, Greece, and
> Asia—and won the pankration events at the
> following festivals: the Olympics at Pisa, in the
> 240th Olympiad [AD 181], and the Pythian
> Games at Delphi; twice at the Isthmian Games;
> twice at the Nemean Games, and also at the
> Shield Games of Hera at Argos; twice at the
> Capitoline Games of Rome; twice at the Eusebia
> Games of Puteoli; and twice at the Sebasta
> Games at Naples.

He also boasted that some of his opponents bowed out as soon as they knew they had to face him. In his midtwenties, he retired, then was drawn back into competition and trounced his opponents yet again at the Alexandrian Games.

The caption of this 1715 drawing of Epictetus: "I was Epictetus the slave, and not sound in all my limbs, and poor as Irus, and beloved by the gods." Irus is the beggar in book 18 of The Odyssey.

Yet the odds of succeeding were always long. The Stoic philosopher Epictetus, who lived in the first century AD, gave this advice to an aspiring athlete:

> *You say you want to be an Olympic champion. But wait. Think about what is involved. . . . You will have to hand your body over to your coach just as you would to a doctor. You will have to obey every instruction. You will have to give up sweet desserts, and eat only at fixed times, no matter how hot or cold the weather. You will be forbidden to drink chilled water. Even wine will be limited. Then, in the contests, you must gouge and be gouged. There will be times that you will sprain a wrist, twist your ankle, swallow mouthfuls of sand and be flogged. And even after that you will probably lose!*

One of the most famous of all ancient superstars was a wrestler of legendary strength named Milo of Croton, whom no one could overpower. As a young man, he began to build up his strength by "hoisting a calf onto his shoulders, and continued to do this as the calf grew into a full-sized ox." Eventually, it was said, he could hold the ox over his head. He had been victorious in the boys' wrestling competition at Olympia in 540 BC, excelled thereafter in every bout, and altogether won six Olympic crowns. He was so feared that in one of the Olympic Games, all those slated to face him withdrew.

Next to Milo in esteem was a mighty boxer named Theagenes of Thasos, who enjoyed an undefeated career over the course of twenty-two years. In some thirteen

A painting of the renowned wrestling champion Milo of Croton, by Joseph-Benoît Suvée, from the eighteenth century.

hundred bouts, he battered his opponents to a pulp. Other Olympic champions of fame were Leonidas of Rhodes, who won three footraces in four consecutive Games, and a long jumper named Phailos, who in 336 BC jumped fifty-five feet and landed with such frightful violence that his splintered shins were driven up into his knees!

Some reported feats of prodigious strength and skill may be myths. But one cannot always be sure. Archaeologists, for example, found a red sandstone boulder at Olympia weighing 315 pounds with an ancient inscription that claimed that a certain strongman named Bybon "threw it over his head with one hand." On the island of Santorini, a volcanic block weighing more than a thousand pounds also turned up with a similar inscription (dated to 500 BC).

Few boxers could get through their careers without being badly mauled. One who evidently did was a boxer by the name of Melankomas, who made his name during the first century AD. He was a boxer of supreme skill. One might compare him to the modern boxer Muhammad Ali, who (as he memorably described himself) could "float like a butterfly, sting like a bee." People who didn't know about Melankomas's past but knew he was a champion thought he must have been a runner, because he was more or less unscarred. Since an ancient boxing match was not limited to a given number of rounds but was one long round until one of the fighters won (usually by a knockout), it was an extreme test of endurance. To increase his staying power, Melankomas would hold his arms up for hours on end—according to one account, up to two days at a time.

One of the great pankration fighters was a man named Polydamas, who prevailed at the Olympiad in 408 BC. An early Greek historian tells us that Polydamas was "the biggest man of his times." He was said to have killed a lion with his bare hands, stopped a chariot in full course, and snapped off the horns of a bull. His own death was heroic. He was attending a party in a cave when the roof

A restored view of the Temple of Zeus at Olympia, painted in 1908.

began to sag. He held it up just long enough for the others to escape before it gave way completely and crushed him under debris.

Yet in ancient Greek culture, Olympic strength itself was not always blindly admired. Milo of Croton, for example, was sometimes made fun of because, though a big man, he was said to have a little brain. It may be true, for he met his end by a dim-witted act. One day when out walking in the forest, he "came across a tree that woodcutters had tried to split, leaving wedges driven into its trunk." The woodcutters had abandoned their task and gone home. But Milo could not resist trying to finish the job. He pulled the trunk apart enough for the wedges to fall out, only to have it close back in and trap his hands. Unable to move, he was eaten that night by wolves.

In addition to being sports spectaculars, the early Olympic Games were also religious festivals held in honor of Zeus, the supreme god of Greek mythology.

Well-known philosophers like Plato (left) and Aristotle (right) attended the Games to observe the competition, as well as to mingle with artists, writers, and other celebrities of the day. (c. 1508)

A trip to Olympia included a solemn visit to his shrine, where pilgrims beheld a forty-foot-high statue, carved in marble, of the great bearded god sitting on an enormous cedar throne. In ancient times, this colossal statue—reflected in a great standing pool of oil—was considered one of the Seven Wonders of the World. The temple itself was adorned with sculptured scenes from Greek mythology and the whole building complex brightly painted in rainbow hues.

Pagan priests presided over the Olympic extravaganza, and as part of their ritual celebrations, they sacrificed oxen and pigs on an altar to the gods. It was also their role to crown the winners of the Games with wreaths of wild olive leaves.

Over the course of five days, there was feasting and pageantry, sideshows and parties, with some pretty wild goings-on. It was a big social occasion. Famous people came to the Games not only for the events themselves but to network and flaunt their own gifts. Aristotle, Socrates, Plato, Herodotus, and other philosophers and writers showed up. Sculptors did, too, and their art was sometimes on display in the form of relief carvings, statues, and busts.

At high noon on the third day of the Games, a herd of bulls was sacrificed, butchered, roasted, and fed to the crowds.

In 146 BC, the Romans appropriated the Olympic Games from the Greeks (whom they had conquered), but in the process the religious character of the Games was lost. By then, scandal and greed had also begun to affect the way the Games were run. The facilities on the whole were improved—an athletes' clubhouse, for example, was added—but more often than before, it was discovered that

An 1878 painting of Emperor Nero titled The Remorse of Nero After the Murder of His Mother, *by John William Waterhouse.*

a judge had been bribed or that some athlete had thrown a match. In time, a carnival atmosphere came to color the Games as a whole. The list of outstanding Olympic performers dwindled, as did the number of stories, poems, and statues to celebrate what they did. The farcical performance of the emperor Nero is often singled out as emblematic of this decline. In AD 67, Nero insisted on taking part in the chariot race. He was unqualified to compete, however, and he blundered at the start, falling off his chariot and landing in a heap of dust on the ground. That should have been the end of it, but he was determined to be the victor and bribed the judges to give him the crown.

In general, the Games were coarsened, and some events came to resemble gladiatorial bouts. As if the contests weren't already rough enough, boxers inserted inch-long metal spikes between the leather straps they wound around their hands. This was not officially sanctioned, and, as one scholar, Thomas F. Scanlon, points out, it turned the match into a street fight—like the knife fights then common in the slums of Rome. The bouts were also held in grueling conditions, in the dog days of August under a scorching Mediterranean sun.

The ancients seemed to have been somewhat self-conscious about the fierceness, if not brutality, of some of the contests and explained them in different ways. Some commended them as exhibitions of strength and skill. Plato looked upon athletic exercise as contributing to civic virtue by creating wholesome men. He believed, as did many, that a healthy body helped create a sound mind—*mens sana in corpore sano,* in the well-known Latin phrase.

Still others—in the spirit of the hoplite race that brought the Games to a close—saw them as a form of military training. When a wrestler struggled "to grab hold of a muddied opponent," he was not only trying to defeat him but also practicing "the dexterity required to rescue a stricken comrade in the thick of the fray." And, the argument ran, "sprinting on soft sand creates stamina for running on hard ground; discus-throwing puts shield-bearing muscle on the shoulders; exercising naked in the midday sun builds endurance; and so on." In that view, the larger aim of athletic contests was to simulate "the stress of battle; to stay sharp and ready for war." Since the ancient Greek word for courage is *andreia,* which means "manliness," some saw the larger objective of the Games as creating courageous men.

Plato was one of those who subscribed to this. In his *Laws,* he talked about the relation of athletics to military skill. He thought that wrestling was useful in preparation for real fighting; that shadowboxing, or pretend combat, helped develop quick reflexes; and that, in order to build up his strength, an athlete should work out once a month in full battle gear.

But others insisted athletics had little or no connection to the real experience of war. "I take no account of a man for his prowess at running or wrestling," wrote one Spartan in the seventh century BC. "No man is good in war unless he can stomach the sight of slaughter and is able, at close quarters, to attack. That kind of courage is what true excellence is made of. It is the utmost that a young man can aspire to and deserves the greatest praise. For when a man holds his ground while fighting in the front ranks—risking his life, displaying a steady spirit, and whispering encouragement to the man at his side"—it benefits the state and the people as a whole.

Two hundred years later, the great Athenian dramatist Euripides expressed his own doubts about the military value of formal athletic training but took the opposite point of view. He argued that those who promoted the arts of peace were especially deserving of acclaim. Specialized athletes, he wrote,

The inscriptions on this second-century statue of the Greek dramatist Euripides list his works.

> *don't really know the world. They cannot survive true privation and are so caught up in their rigid exercise routines that they can't adapt when hardships arrive. They strut about in their prime, infatuated with their own youth and fitness, but when bitter old age descends, they fall apart like worn-out clothes. I deplore the custom of lionizing these types. . . . What good does a community actually get from someone winning a big wrestling match? What good does it really get from someone who happens to have nimble feet, or can lob a discus, or deal out a neat right hook? Will they go into battle armed*

with a discus, or break through a wall of enemy
shields with their fists? It is foolish to compare
sports to real battle. . . . Better to award laurels
to those who remain good, honorable men
through thick and thin, who devote themselves
with integrity to public service, and who use
their wisdom and eloquence to steer their
communities away from unnecessary war.

Centuries later, during the Roman civil war, Julius Caesar told his own troops before a big battle that some of the soldiers in the ranks of his opponent would be pushovers, because they were mere athletes trained in gymnasiums and wouldn't know how to fight.

Perhaps the analogy of sport to war was never meant to be taken literally anyway, even by some of its advocates. To some, indeed, it was simply the sheer ferocity of the Games that made no sense. One Roman orator named Lucian, who lived in the second century AD, imagined a time traveler going back to ancient Greece and thinking the Greeks must have been out of their minds to compete as they did—"tripping each other up, attacking each other with kicks and blows, choking and twisting each other, and groveling in the mud like swine."

After the Roman Empire officially adopted Christianity in AD 324, the worship of the old pagan gods, including Zeus, Hera, Apollo, and Poseidon, was condemned. A series of edicts was issued against offering libations at pagan altars and sacrificing animals to the gods to win their favor. As a result, the festivities at Olympia began to wind down. While Christians on the whole condemned the Olympics, King Herod of Judaea (the arch-villain of the New Testament) was a fan of the Games and in 12 BC rescued them from financial ruin with a big donation from his treasure chest.

At the same time, ironically enough, the writings of early Christians facing persecution often used the language of the Games to express their plight. This was because athletics and suffering were often closely linked. After all, ascetics "trained" like athletes, and both were prominent in the ancient world. The letters of Saint Paul in the New Testament, for example, urged his fellow Christians "to fight the good fight," "to finish the course," and to gain "the crown of righteousness" in their struggle with sin. Saint Paul called Christ himself the "forerunner," meaning "the one who sets the pace in a race." Martyrs were praised as "athletes of Christ," and even the bearded figure of Zeus that overawed visitors to his shrine became the image of Christ Pantocrator (Christ as ruler of the universe) in the iconography of the church.

The two ideas—agony and sport—were also oddly joined in a passage from the Roman historian Tacitus, who mentions that the emperor Nero made Christians the scapegoats for a fire that devastated Rome in AD 64. Some, he tells us, were "arrested. Then, on their information, large numbers of others were condemned. . . . Dressed in wild-animal skins, they were torn to pieces by dogs, or crucified, or made into torches to be ignited after dark as substitutes for daylight." Nero presided over all this as if he were attending an Olympic extravaganza at the Circus Maximus, the official sports stadium, "standing in a chariot, dressed as a charioteer"!

In short, the Olympics were woven into the very fabric of the ancient world. But by the end of the fourth century

AD, they had also had their day. Year by year, Christian condemnation took its toll. So it was that after a long decline in public esteem, the Games—which had continued in an unbroken chain for a thousand years—were abolished by the Roman emperor Theodosius I in AD 394. Some thirty years later, the Temple of Zeus burned down, and other pagan temples throughout the eastern Mediterranean were destroyed.

Nature took care of the rest. Beginning in the fifth century AD, earthquakes toppled buildings connected to the Olympic stadium and shrine, and floods from the Alpheus River washed away the hippodrome.

For fourteen hundred years, Olympia itself would lie buried deep beneath mud and silt.

.

CHAPTER THREE

The New Olympic Movement

Yet the memory of the Games endured. In the early Middle Ages, the Byzantine (or East Roman) Empire tried for a time to re-create them and built a vast hippodrome for the chariot race in Constantinople, the seat of imperial power. But the Byzantine Games were a poor imitation of what had been.

In seventeenth-century England, an annual sports festival known as the Cotswold Olimpick Games emerged, but they were Olympic in name only and lasted for just a stretch of about thirty years. The main events were sledgehammer throwing, sack jumping, shin kicking, cudgel fighting, and dancing, mixed in with horse racing, wrestling, and other traditional sports. Started in 1612 by a local Cotswold lawyer, Robert Dover, with the blessing of King James, the Games took place on the Thursday and Friday of Whitsun Week (which fell between mid-May and mid-June) above the town of Chipping Campden, in Gloucestershire. Tents were erected for the gentry, who came from counties all around, and everyone wore festive yellow ribbons pinned to their hats and clothes. A temporary wooden battlement,

A woodcut poster advertising the 1636 Cotswold Games.

known playfully as Dover Castle, was set up in a valley enclosed by gentle hills. At the sound of a hunting horn, competitors would assemble to take part in various sports, and small mounted cannons were fired to signal the start of the events. Officials called sticklers served as referees, and silver trophies and other prizes were handed out. (That, by the way, is where we get our phrase "a stickler for the rules.") An entertainer dressed as the poet Homer went among the crowds strumming a harp, and in keeping with the classical theme, there was a maze known as Troy Town, constructed from piled-up turf. A good deal of gambling—backgammon, chess, and cards—went on behind the scenes for small stakes. King James, incidentally, approved of card games "when you have no other thing ado . . . and are weary of reading . . . and when it is foul and stormy weather," but he considered chess to be "too obsessive a game." The Games ended with a flurry of fireworks and patriotic songs.

All in all, the Cotswold Olimpicks resembled a county fair far more than the ancient Olympic Games. Demonstrations of athletic prowess were not their main intent. They enjoyed royal support because King James thought they would promote goodwill among the common people toward their monarch. Bringing rich and poor together, he thought, might also help ease social tensions by bridging class divides.

The Games caught on. The English poet Ben Jonson, for example, saw them as good for the public spirit and a positive release of energy in old-fashioned fun. Others, however, disapproved—in particular, the English Puritans, who looked down on any carefree, festive celebrations (including dancing and even a little drinking) as the Devil's work. The fact that the Cotswold fair took place on a church holiday such as Whitsun made it worse. At the time, the king and his supporters were at odds with the Puritans over many issues, and hostility between them increased over the course of many years. Eventually, it resulted in the outbreak of the English Civil War in 1642. The Puritans won and cut off the king's head, and the Cotswold Games were banned. But after the restoration of the monarchy in 1660, they were revived. As if to prove the Puritans right, however, the Games proceeded to degenerate into a drunken and disorderly spectacle. They also took on a nasty streak. In the shin-kicking contests, for example, the competitors wore heavily nailed boots, sometimes with pointed tips. One writer in 1740 described the Games as ending in a general brawl in which people threw bottles at one another and broke chairs.

Meanwhile, across the English Channel in France, the Olympics were briefly revived (1796 to 1798) in the form of a single running event. By then, other develop-

King James I of England supported the Cotswold Games as an opportunity to improve his public image and to bridge class divides.

ments had begun to take shape that would lead to the Games' return. To begin with, the Renaissance (1400 to 1600)—a tremendous period of scholarship and study that followed the Middle Ages—had led to a revival of classical learning. One of the offshoots of this study was a renewed interest in the anatomy and structure of the human body—often vividly exhibited in ancient works of art. Physicians in England, Sweden, Germany, and elsewhere began to think in a more scientific way about the relationship of exercise to health and the impact of running, jumping, climbing, and vaulting on the development of tissue, muscle, and bone.

At first, ancient Latin, or Roman, culture was all the rage. But in the eighteenth century, a Greek revival led by a German schoolmaster named Johann Winckelmann revealed that many Roman works of art were modeled on Greek originals. After Winckelmann published his extremely influential *History of Ancient Art* in 1764, the whole of Europe was seized with a fever of curiosity about ancient Greece. Poets experimented with Greek verse forms, architects incorporated Greek porticoes and

colonnades into their buildings, painters were inspired by Greek themes, and even furniture makers imitated ancient Greek styles in their tables and chairs. Not surprisingly, archaeologists were eager to uncover whatever might remain of famous building sites from the classical past. And so it was that in 1766 the Olympic sanctuary was discovered by Richard Chandler, a scholar from Oxford University in England. He went to Olympia as part of an expedition to see what he could find. With the help of a Turkish guide, Chandler picked his way through fields of cotton shrubs and thistles, crossed a shallow brook, and emerged into a broad clearing, where he found a stagnant pool alongside some tumbledown pillars and shattered facades and walls. Brushing aside clouds of gnats, he took out a notebook and began to record what he saw.

In subsequent years, more adventurers followed—some in search of statues and other artifacts, others to sketch or paint the scene. But no actual excavation was done until 1829, when French archaeologists unearthed part of the Temple of Zeus and a handful of sculptured reliefs.

A 1768 portrait of Johann Winckelmann, the famed German art historian and proponent of the Greek revival that took place in the late eighteenth and early nineteenth centuries.

A contemporary view of Dover's Hill, site of the Cotswold Games.

Baron Pierre de Coubertin was an important early champion of the Olympic Movement in the late nineteenth century. (c. 1915)

It was the Germans who really got down to work in the nineteenth century to dig things up. Beginning in 1875, Otto von Bismarck, Germany's first chancellor, committed government funds to the project, and over the course of the next six years, the clear outlines of the stadium, the hippodrome, the Temple of Zeus, and other sites emerged. One unexpected find was an exquisite marble statue of Hermes (the messenger of the gods) playing with a child. Such discoveries inspired public nostalgia for the glory of ancient times.

Meanwhile, with the development of general and public education, many countries began to recognize the importance of physical exercise, especially for the young. This combination of nostalgia for an ideal past and renewed interest in athletic fitness gave rise to the Olympic Movement—the idea of fostering international goodwill through rivalry in sports. The movement had a number of proponents, but its main champion was a French aristocrat, Baron Pierre de Coubertin.

From an early age, Coubertin took a keen interest in collegiate athletics and was a firm believer in the parallel development of body and mind. He believed in amateur competitions (in which unpaid athletes strove only to prove their excellence), while his imagination was also fired by stories of the ancient Olympic Truce. At the very least, the idea of the truce created a precedent for harmonious competition between otherwise hostile states.

Coubertin was fascinated by the idea that the Olympics might have a role in advancing peace. He hoped through athletic competition to promote international cooperation and even reduce the threat of war. In his own mind, the competition itself was more important than winning, and he imagined (falsely) that the ancient Greeks had shared this ideal. He wrote, "The important thing in life is not the triumph but the struggle . . . not to have conquered but to have fought well."

Coubertin's notions were undoubtedly influenced by his genteel and privileged upbringing. Born in Paris on January 1, 1863, he could trace his noble lineage back to the early fifteenth century, when members of his family became part of the French ruling elite. Perhaps his interest in the classical past was also stimulated by his father, a prominent painter whose work dealt with themes and ideas borrowed from the history of Greece and Rome. At the same time, even as a boy, Coubertin had been concerned about the anger and animosities that seemed to exist between peoples and states. Indeed, his acute longing for peace was a reaction to the political and social turmoil of the times in which he lived.

His own country of France, for example, was going through a profound period of change. It had recently experienced humiliating defeat in the Franco-Prussian War (1870 to 1871), followed by a prolonged struggle to establish a stable regime. In the midst of this strife, his parents sent him to a Jesuit school, hoping a strong moral and religious education would make him into an upstanding young man.

He responded well to the training, excelled in class, and upon graduation enjoyed unlimited prospects. As a wealthy and well-connected aristocrat, he could have any career he wished. No doubt his parents expected him to carve out a place for himself among the military or political elite. But by nature he was something of a scholar, with a contemplative turn of mind. He chose to explore and write about a broad range of topics, but above all he was interested in what today we call physical education. He believed that civilized sport helped create a balanced personality, with a healthy equilibrium between body and mind. In his opinion, the ancient Greek gymnasium had done just that. Of course, his idea of ancient Greek Olympic sport was idealized, for he pictured it as a sort of gentlemanly competition and not the bloody, brutal combination of contests it really was.

Another of Coubertin's mistaken ideas was that the ancient Olympics had encouraged competition among amateur rather than professional athletes. That assumed that only young gentlemen (that is, men of means) had been allowed to compete, their strivings unsullied by cash. If that had been proper for the Greeks, it was proper for modern athletes, too.

As a student of history, Coubertin managed to deceive himself, for he imagined the past as he would have liked it to have been. In other words, he saw it through romantic eyes. The nineteenth century was a period of Romanticism, and he, like many others, pictured the Greco-Roman world as a golden age. He convinced himself that its culture had been not only high but unblemished and that its heroes represented the utmost that human nature could achieve. Even those who might not have described themselves as Romantics were profoundly influenced by Romantic thinking. This was so in America as well as Europe; one exquisite expression of it may be found in Edgar Allan Poe's poem "To Helen," written to a woman he loved. He describes her as an image of statuesque perfection whose "classic face" and refined nature

brought me home
To the glory that was Greece,
And the grandeur that was Rome.

Romanticism prized ancient civilizations like Greece and Rome and influenced many literary, musical, and artistic creations of Coubertin's time.

Coubertin's idea of a modern Olympics did the same for him.

Coubertin's fanciful theories about the classical world merged with a fascination he came to have with the British public school system (which is actually a system of private schools), where notions of the character-forming power of sport played a prominent role. He was especially impressed by the wholesome traditional values inculcated in the students at a school called Rugby, which had long been led by an educator named Thomas Arnold. Arnold's system was featured in a famous novel called *Tom Brown's School Days*, which Coubertin had avidly read. In some ways, Rugby came to define by its example what an English public school was supposed to be.

Thomas Arnold was one of Coubertin's heroes. Coubertin believed that public school training cultivated an "athletic chivalry" that had contributed to the growth of the British civil servant class. That class had come to staff, rather successfully, a huge expansion of the British Empire.

After Coubertin went to England to visit Rugby and other English schools, he wrote a book titled *Education in England,* in which he concluded that "organized sport can create moral and social strength." To help advance his ideas, he united sports enthusiasts from all over France in one association and founded a monthly magazine called *La Revue Athlétique* (*The Athletic Review*). Over the course of just a few years, the French athletic association grew

Edgar Allan Poe

Ludwig van Beethoven

The Wanderer Above the Sea of Fog *by Caspar David Friedrich*

Pride and Prejudice *by Jane Austen*

rapidly, from seven sporting societies with approximately eight hundred members to sixty-two societies with seven thousand members by 1892. Meanwhile, gentlemen's sports clubs were formed on both sides of the Atlantic as the momentum for the revival of the Olympic Games began to mature.

Thomas Arnold was not the only important influence on Coubertin. William Penny Brookes, a physician who believed that physical exercise was the key to moral and physical health, impressed him, too. In 1850, Brookes founded the Wenlock Olympian Society at Much Wenlock in Shropshire, England, which held a little festival of annual games that were supposed to promote "the moral, physical, and intellectual improvement" of those who took part. A few of the games were athletic or Olympic in the traditional sense. Others were more or less English country sports, like cricket and quoits (a form of horseshoes).

In time, Brookes joined forces with the Liverpool Athletic Club (which had begun holding its own "Olympic Festival" in the 1860s) to create the National Olympian Association, aimed at fostering local competition in cities across the land. At first, the British sporting establishment looked down on this initiative. But then it began to catch on. Meanwhile, Brookes made contact with the government in Greece and proposed the idea of reviving the Olympic Games under the auspices of the Greek government. In Greece itself, a national interest in reviving the Olympic Games had also started to take hold. It began with the Greek war of independence from the Ottoman Empire in 1821 and was subsequently pushed by some wealthy Greek philanthropists. The ancient Panathenaic Stadium in Athens was restored as a site for future Olym-

The Panathenaic Stadium in Athens was restored in the late seventeenth century and is still in use today.

pic Games; all-Greek Olympics were held there in 1870 and 1875 before sizable crowds.

In short, a great many developments began to converge. Just at this time Brookes wrote to Coubertin in 1890, and they began an animated dialogue about education and sport. That October, Brookes invited Coubertin to a festival held in his honor at Much Wenlock, and from then on the two joined forces to realize a common goal. But it was Coubertin who took the lead as he pressed his case for reviving the Olympics among sports enthusiasts in France, Britain, and the United States.

On June 23, 1894, an Olympic congress was convened at the Sorbonne University in Paris, and out of it emerged plans for a festival of games to be held every four years (as in ancient Greece). The International Olympic Committee was formed with a Greek as its first head, and the first Games were scheduled to take place in Athens in 1896. It was also agreed that only unpaid amateurs, not professionals, would be allowed to take part.

With understandable pride and satisfaction, Coubertin saw his cherished goal at last within reach. "The Olympic idea," he eloquently declared, "has traversed the mists of the ages like an all-powerful ray of sunlight and returned to illumine the threshold of the twentieth century with a gleam of joyous hope."

CHAPTER FOUR

Uncertain Footing

On April 6, 1896, the anniversary of Greek independence and the day after Easter, the first of the modern Olympic Games was opened at the Panathenaic Stadium in Athens

The Panathenaic Stadium on the first day of the 1896 Olympics.

before a capacity crowd of eighty thousand—perhaps the largest crowd ever to witness a sporting event. The timing could hardly have been more auspicious, being tied to the date of the Resurrection, and in regal splendor King George I of Greece presided, flanked by his wife and sons.

Two hundred forty-one athletes from fourteen nations gathered to compete in forty-three events, and if not quite as international as Coubertin had hoped, the Games had made a start. The Panathenaic Stadium, constructed in the fourth century BC and subsequently expanded and adorned with marble by the Roman emperor Hadrian, had just the right antique character and atmosphere to conjure up the athletic glories of the past.

The Games themselves were somewhat improvised, and the kinds of events deemed suitable took some sorting out. It was proposed, for example, that they include mountain climbing, choral singing, aesthetic dancing, fishing, and lawn bowling. But the main attraction proved to be the track-and-field events—the footraces, pole vault, shot put, discus throw, broad jump, high jump, and marathon. These all came under the heading of "athletics"—as distinct from cycling, fencing, shooting, swimming, tennis, wrestling, and the like. That way of categorizing sports events might seem strange. After all, all sports contests are athletic in some sense. But in time, the term came to apply more narrowly to any kind of running (or walking), jumping, or throwing event—in short, track and field.

The first champion of the modern Games was a Harvard dropout named James B. Connolly (later a famous writer of sea tales), who won the triple jump event (hop, skip, and jump). Greece had been favored to win the discus throw and the shot put but finished just behind the Americans in both events. No world records were set, but the French and Greeks excelled in fencing, the Germans in gymnastics (which included the horizontal bar, parallel bars, and vault), and the Swiss on the pommel horse. Two American brothers, John and Sumner Paine, prevailed as marksmen in the military pistols competition (the first siblings to rank in the same event), but the Greeks won in the military rifle contest with a perfect score. In keeping with ideals of sportsmanship, a Frenchman, Léon Flameng, won the 100-kilometer cycling race despite politely stopping to wait for his Greek opponent to fix a mechanical problem with one of his gears.

Nothing went quite right with the swimming competitions (100-, 500-, and 1,200-meter freestyle), which were held in the open sea, for the water was too cold and turbulent to race in. Nearly twenty thousand spectators thronged the coast off Piraeus (the port of Athens) to watch, only to see their favorite swimmers bobbing like buoys in the waves. On the other hand, the one-armed weight-lifting event proved an unexpected draw. It was won by a handsome, dashing Scot named Launceston Elliot, who was wildly popular with the women in the crowd. In the two-handed lifting event, Elliot tied with a Dane but placed second in style. In the course of the contest, Greek national pride got a welcome boost. The crown prince of Greece happened to be in attendance and stepped in to help an official who wasn't strong enough to remove some weights. Like Odysseus of old, he nonchalantly picked one up and cast it off to the side.

But the sentimental hero of the Games was a Greek shepherd, a spindly little fellow named Spyridon Louis,

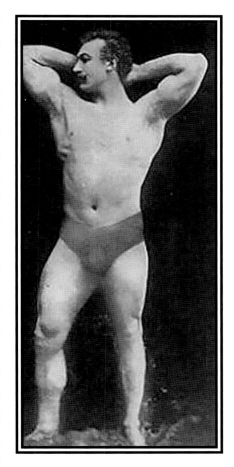

The Scottish weight lifter Launceston Elliot was a crowd-pleaser in the 1896 Games.

The Greek shepherd Spyridon Louis placed first in the 1896 Olympic marathon after two days of fasting and prayer.

who won the twenty-six-mile marathon after two days of fasting and prayer. It was almost as if the history of the Games had come full circle back to their humble beginning, when the first footrace was won by a cook.

The marathon, however, was a modern innovation. Long-distance running had not been recognized in ancient Greece as a competitive sport. Rather, the race commemorated a celebrated moment in the Greek past. In 490 BC, the city of Marathon was the site of a great battle between the Persians and the Greeks. Against all odds, the outnumbered Greeks won. A Greek runner named Pheidippides was dispatched from Marathon to Athens (about twenty-five miles away) to announce the triumph and ran the distance without stopping. But no sooner did he deliver his message ("We were victorious!") than he collapsed and died. Thanks to the modern marathon, the word has come to be synonymous with a long-distance run.

In the end, most of the nations taking part earned medals and came away satisfied. The United States and Greece were the biggest winners overall.

The Greeks did so well in part because they had by far the largest team. Their athletes were also more diverse. All the American athletes were from Ivy League schools, and all the British from Oxford and Cambridge—in keeping with the genteel amateur ideal. The British even tried to prevent two members of their own team from competing in the cycling race because they were paid, if unofficial, members of the British diplomatic staff.

Women were not allowed to compete in any of the contests, even though they had been accorded some role in ancient times. Perhaps this was simply because in the nineteenth century, women were generally excluded from many activities—and the idea of a female athlete was considered strange. But as times changed, so did attitudes about the involvement of women in sports and other fields. Before long, the Games would begin to include them, though in a subordinate role.

Once the week of Games concluded, the king threw a great banquet for the athletes and officials and handed out awards. Spyridon Louis, winner of the marathon, led the medalists on a victory lap around the stadium before the crowd dispersed. The Olympic gold medal, by the way, had not yet been established, so the first-place winners each received a silver medal, a diploma, and an olive branch. (Since that time, gold, silver, and bronze medals have been retroactively awarded to the three best-placed athletes in each event.)

The medal handed to winners at the 1896 Games.

Following the success of the 1896 Games, the Olympics entered a period of stagnation that threatened their survival. The ancient Games had been sensationally popular—the greatest recurring event in antiquity for over a thousand years. By contrast, the modern Games had some trouble gaining traction with fans.

Though the Athens contests proved a spur to the Greek economy—and gave a lift to Greek pride—Coubertin had hoped they would do more to promote the Olympic idea. The Games held four years later in Paris, in conjunction with the 1900 Paris World's Fair, were even more of a letdown, because the fair itself completely overshadowed

A poster announcing the second modern Olympics at the Paris World's Fair in 1900.

the Olympic events. The director of the fair, Alfred Picard, thought that featuring ancient sport events at the fair was an "absurd anachronism" that went against the whole spirit of the "modern" that the fair was supposed to represent. He was so intent on downplaying the Olympic concept that he failed to provide a stadium for the competitions and eliminated the phrase "Olympic Games" from the program of the fair. Instead, the Games were obscurely advertised as "international physical exercises and sports."

As a result, there were no opening or closing ceremonies, and a week's worth of events was stretched out over five and a half months—May 14 to October 28—more or less the span of the fair itself. That robbed them of the separate identity they required. This was too bad, because over a thousand competitors from twenty-four countries took part in nineteen different sports. A good cross section of traditional sports was worked into the program, including track-and-field athletics, swimming, wrestling, gymnastics, fencing, boxing, yacht racing, and cycling. Others, such as archery, rowing, diving, rugby (a style of football developed at Rugby School in England), water polo, and a tug-of-war event, made their debut. The "unofficial" sports offered included angling (fishing), ballooning, cannon shooting, firefighting, kite flying, lifesaving, lawn tennis, motorcycle racing, pigeon racing, and Basque pelota (also known as jai alai). In a breakthrough, two women's events were included: tennis and croquet. In tennis, Charlotte Cooper of England, already a star as a three-time Wimbledon champion, won both the singles and mixed doubles to become the first female Olympic champion. A seven-year-old boy, weighing just under seventy-three pounds, helped the Dutch rowing team to prevail.

The English tennis player Charlotte Cooper, seen here in 1900, was the first female Olympic champion.

In other milestones (more or less unnoticed at the time), the Franco-Haitian rugby center Constantin Henriquez de Zubiera became the first black medalist, and Alvin Kraenzlein of the United States won four medals and virtually swept the track and field—taking the

60-meter sprint, the 110-meter hurdles, the 200-meter hurdles, and the long jump. After his victory in the long jump, however, he was punched in the face by a teammate, Meyer Prinstein, who had been denied the chance to compete in the final by officials of his Christian university because it was a Sunday event. One can understand his frustration. He was Jewish, and Sunday wasn't his "day of rest." Moreover, the two teammates had had an informal agreement not to compete on Sunday if either was barred. When Prinstein learned that Kraenzlein had betrayed him, he became enraged. The following day, he proved he had the right stuff and won the gold medal in the triple jump.

Other competitions did little to enhance the reputation of the Games. An uneven meadow cut by a ditch was made to serve as a track, and the swimming events were held in the muddy waters of the Seine. There was also a weird underwater obstacle course race that required contestants to swim under and climb over rows of boats. And the rowing competition, also held on the Seine, descended into chaos when officials kept changing the rules. For

The Seine, shown here in 1870, runs through Paris and was the site of the swimming competitions at the 1900 Games.

sheer thematic reasons, the fencing competition was held in a field near the fair's cutlery exhibit; since the first rounds were scored on style rather than hits, some of the fencers who had clearly lost were advanced. Finally, only two teams played in the cricket tournament, and a single paying spectator attended the final in croquet.

No contest spawned more ill will, however, than the marathon, which was run along a confused course through the Bois de Boulogne. Some runners lost their way; others, baffled by slanted signs, took alternate routes; still others struggled to thread through throngs of cars, bicycles, pedestrians, and dogs. One American runner swore he had been knocked down by a cyclist; another that no one ever passed him in the race. The Frenchman who won—possibly by taking a shortcut—turned out to be not from France but from Luxembourg.

Hardly anyone paid attention anyway. The Paris World's Fair had been staged on a grand scale to celebrate the achievements of the past century and those hoped for in the next. It hosted more than seventy-six thousand exhibitors, covered almost a square mile, and attracted more than fifty million people. Unlike most fairs, many of its buildings were built to last—among them some train stations and museums that remain part of Paris today. The first line of the Paris metro, or subway, was launched to coincide with the fair, and the design of the metro kiosks (entranceways and exits) helped announce a new architectural and artistic style known as Art Nouveau. The fair also introduced escalators, the diesel engine (which ran on peanut oil), and the first films projected with recorded sound. The largest refracting telescope in the world was likewise on display. Finally, there was the Exhibit of American Negroes, conceived and developed by Booker T. Washington and W. E. B. DuBois, both prominent in the struggle for equal rights. African Americans had been a part of the Chicago World's Fair of 1893 and viewed the Paris fair as another opportunity to demonstrate their worth. After all, it had been only thirty-five years since

Booker T. Washington (top, date unknown) and W. E. B. DuBois (bottom, 1946) organized the Exhibit of American Negroes at the Paris World's Fair to highlight the many important contributions to society made by African Americans.

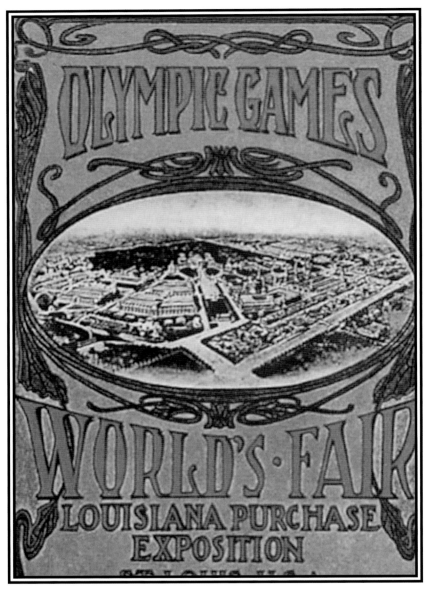

A poster for the 1904 Olympics at the World's Fair in St. Louis, Missouri.

slavery in America had come to an end. On display were many examples of African American ingenuity and know-how, including books, models, maps, patents, drawings, and so on by African Americans.

Just as the Games had proved a sideshow in Paris, they seemed an adjunct to the 1904 World's Fair in St. Louis, Missouri. The United States had just won the Spanish-American War, and the fair was meant to celebrate the emergence of the country as a great power. President Theodore Roosevelt predicted that the twentieth century would be "an American century," and the fair had been conceived to mark the centennial of the Louisiana Purchase, when much of what is now the south-central United States was acquired from the French. Roosevelt's daughter Alice was one of those chosen to officiate. The fair covered twelve hundred acres, making it larger than Chicago's fair of 1893, and there was a classical Greco-Roman look to its white palaces and buildings. Technological innovation was its theme, but it also introduced Americans to iced tea and the ice cream cone. Officially, at least 651 athletes—645 men and six women representing twelve countries—performed. But it was barely international, since most of the athletes were from the United States. Whereas in 1900 the Olympics were unnaturally stretched out, in 1904 they were oddly compressed, held over the course of just a few days—from Monday, August 29, to Saturday, September 3. On the plus side, the three-medal format (gold, silver, and bronze) was introduced; the range of standard events increased—as boxing, dumbbells, freestyle wrestling, and the classic pentathlon made their debuts—and baseball and basketball were offered as demonstration sports.

The start of the 100-meter swimming race at the 1904 Olympics.

Although the venues for some of the events were woefully inadequate—the swimming contests, for example, were held in a scuzzy, polluted green pond that made some of the swimmers sick—at least three records were set. Meyer Prinstein, who had been cheated out of a chance to win gold in the long jump in 1900, returned with a vengeance and won both the long jump and the triple jump on the same day—the only athlete ever to win both events in the same Games. He also came in fifth in both the 60-meter and 400-meter dashes. A Chicago runner, Jim Lightbody, set a world record in the 1,500-meter race. Another American, Archie Hahn, set an Olympic record in the 200-meter that stood for twenty-eight years.

Perhaps because of the haphazard character of the Games, there were a number of anomalies. Women—formally dressed in hats, petticoats, flounced skirts, and long-sleeved blouses—were allowed to compete only in the archery event. The American gymnast George Eyser won six medals, even though his left leg was made of wood. The tug-of-war contest was disgraced when it was discovered that the winning team had brought in unauthorized strongmen to help it prevail. The 50-meter freestyle swimming event had a contested outcome and ended in a fight.

The marathon had all the hallmarks of a sandlot event. The race was run in fiercely hot weather, over dusty mountain roads crowded with cars and horses. Some runners were given sponge baths as they ran. Others were accompanied by their trainers, who rode beside them in cars. Among the thirty-two runners taking part, those representing South Africa had no training whatsoever and just happened to be working at the fair.

The tug-of-war competition at the 1904 Games.

Another man in the lineup was a Cuban postman named Felix Carbajal, who was so poor he had to beg in the streets of Havana for his fare to the United States. He had hitchhiked to St. Louis from the East Coast, joined the marathon at the last minute, and had to run in street shoes and slacks cut down for shorts. In the course of the race, he stopped to shake hands with spectators and even paused in an orchard to feast on some fruit, since he hadn't eaten in two days. The fruit proved rotten, and he was crippled with cramps. After a siesta, however, he rose, continued on, and actually finished fourth!

After encountering a series of obstacles, Cuban runner Feliz Carbajal still managed to finish fourth in the 1904 marathon.

The marathon also included the first black South Africans (two Tswana tribesmen) to compete in the Olympics—though they weren't supposed to be in the race at all. They were part of the Boer War exhibit but had joined the race for fun. Even so, one finished ninth and the other came in twelfth. The first to arrive at the finish line was a man named Frederick Lorz, who had actually dropped out. (After the first nine miles, he had flagged down his manager, who gave him a lift for the rest of the way in his car.) But when he crossed the finish line on foot, he was hailed as the winner. He was soon found out, of course, but the real winner, Thomas Hicks (a Briton running for the United States), deserved the prize even less. He had been doped up by his trainers, who gave him a near-fatal dose of strychnine sulfate mixed with egg yolk and brandy. Unable to cross the line on his own, he had to be supported in the last stretch and was rushed to a hospital, where he spent several days in intensive care.

But scarcely anyone noticed, for the Games were once more lost in the sheer size and variety of the fair itself. The "ethnic exhibits" proved a stronger draw.

Unfortunately, these exhibits had a bigoted cast, for their purpose was to put the so-called primitive peoples of the world on display. Organized by W. J. McGee, who had previously been forced to resign from the Bureau of American Ethnology, the exhibits sought to advance his theory of the superiority of whites in the evolution of the human race. Over two thousand native peoples, including fifty-one American Indian tribes, had been brought to the fair from all over the world.

One of the worst exhibits featured a Philippine village, where a thousand native Igorot tribesmen, dressed in loincloths, could be seen going about their daily lives. From time to time, they were called upon to demonstrate their tribal dances and (according to their custom) publicly kill, roast, and eat dogs. This gruesome sideshow became one of the sensations of the fair.

A group of Pygmies had also been brought over from Africa. One of them was displayed as a cannibal, and to make him look savage, his teeth had been filed to points. After the fair closed, he was exhibited elsewhere around the country and even displayed in a cage at a zoo in New York. There he was forced to live, as if in his "native habitat," with monkeys and apes. Finally, he was sent to an orphanage (merely because he was small, even though he was an adult), where he committed suicide.

If the fair itself was a hit, attendance at the Games was poor. One reason (which also contributed to the shortage of athletes) was the outbreak of the Russo-Japanese War. Despite the ideals of the Olympic Truce, the Games, in fact, were destined to be interrupted more than once by major conflicts, and some of the seeds of future wars were sown at this time.

In the Far East, Russia had been extending its sway down into the Caucasus and Central Asia, while Britain was establishing its hold on India, Upper Burma, Malaysia, North Borneo, and Hong Kong. Meanwhile, Japan, allied with Britain, had transformed itself from a semi-medieval feudal society into a modern, Westernized industrial and military state.

Russia failed to take note. As late as 1903, there wasn't a single general book about Japan in the whole of the Russian Empire. "To most Russians, Japan was a fairy-book sort of place," as one writer put it, "filled with fascinating little people who lived in paper houses . . . and wasted hours on flower arrangement and tea ceremonies."

As tensions rose between the two powers, Russia never expected Japan to go to war. After all, Japan was a newly emergent country, and the Russians thought of the Japanese almost as children, incapable of managing large military equipment because of their smaller size. Aside from greatly underestimating the number of fighting men Japan could muster, the Russians also believed that "one Russian soldier was the equal of three Japanese."

Strengthened by their alliance with Britain, however, the Japanese believed that if war broke out, they could prevail. With world opinion on their side, on February 8, 1904, the Japanese launched a devastating surprise attack on a Russian fleet at anchor in a Manchurian port. The fighting spread, and the sea-and-land war as it developed

A Japanese propaganda poster from 1904 or 1905 shows Czar Nicholas II waking from a nightmare in which the battered military equipment of his Russian forces limps home after being defeated by Japan.

A 1905 poster featuring the envoys
at the Portsmouth Peace Conference:
Komura Jutaro and Kogoro Takahira,
representing Japan; Sergei Witte
and Roman Romanovich Rosen,
representing Russia; and President
Theodore Roosevelt, who served as
mediator.

was enormously costly for both
sides. Two huge battles alone cost
each side over one hundred thousand dead.

At length, President Theodore
Roosevelt arranged a peace conference between the belligerents
at Portsmouth, New Hampshire.
There a deal was struck. But the
hostility between them would
play out over the course of two
world wars.

CHAPTER FIVE

The Games Gain Ground

The 1906 Intercalated Olympic Games were held in this stadium in Athens.

After the fiasco of 1904, the Olympic Movement had to reboot. It needed a recognizable spectacle of Games that could be seen as truly belonging to the tradition it claimed to revive. The Games returned to Athens to find it, and there in 1906—halfway between the usual Games—a one-time intermediate sports festival known as the Intercalated Olympic Games was staged. They were genuinely Olympic in spirit and actually more successful in promoting the movement than anything held since 1896. It was

The crowds arriving at the stadium in Athens.

at these Games that the opening ceremony made its debut as a separate staged event at which, for the first time, the athletes marched into the stadium as national teams, each following its country's flag. It also introduced the closing ceremony and the raising of national flags for those who garnered gold. Though no records were broken, a broad international field of participants took part. Public interest was raised, and the news coverage the event generated helped keep the Olympics alive.

Rome began to prepare for the next great Olympic festival, to take place in 1908. To go from Athens to Rome seemed the perfect way to evoke the classical heritage of sport. But scarcely had the necessary funds been collected when Mount Vesuvius erupted and nearly wiped the city of Naples off the map. The top of the mountain blew off, rivers of hot molten lava flowed down its sides, and great columns of volcanic ash spewed thousands of feet into the air. All the resources earmarked for the Olympics had to be diverted to the city's rescue, and subsequent reconstruction soaked up whatever else might have been raised. Though London volunteered to host the Games instead, that was seen as a gamble, for it would mean that they would once more be held in conjunction with an international fair. In this case, the fair was the Franco-British Exhibition, which was put together to celebrate the new political alliance recently forged between Britain and France.

As with the fair of 1904, the London exhibition featured two colonial villages—Irish and Senegalese—designed to demonstrate how native peoples prospered under colonial rule. The Irish village (called Ballymaclinton) was inhabited by 150 "colleens," or Irish girls, who could be observed, as in a diorama, going about their various domestic tasks. The Senegalese village (like the Philippine village in St. Louis) was a so-called native village showing the people in their "habitat." Some visitors were

The Dutch gymnastics team at the 1908 Olympic Games.

The White City Stadium in London, the site of the 1908 Games.

evidently surprised to discover that the Irish and the Senegalese paid any attention to hygiene.

But this time around, the Olympic Games also got the attention they deserved. Twenty-two sports were featured, including tennis, shooting (pistol, shotgun, and rifle), fencing, rowing, polo, boxing, diving, swimming, water polo, figure skating, jeu de paume (a form of tennis, using the hands), sailing, archery, track and field, cycling, field hockey, soccer, gymnastics, lacrosse, rugby, tug-of-war, and wrestling.

Some twenty-one nations took part, and the king of England, Edward VII, presided over the impressive opening ceremonies, which helped ensure the Games would not be shunted to the side. Moreover, a great White City, as it was called, with its own large stadium, was built for the occasion in an area of West London known as Shepherd's Bush. The White City—named for its white marble cladding—covered some 140 acres and included a large artificial lake surrounded by a building complex.

As always, there was some controversy. Before the start of the Games, the various teams paraded into the stadium behind their national flags. The Swedes boycotted this event because their flag had not been raised atop the stadium with the others at the outset. The Finns refused to march in under the Russian flag to protest Russian occupation of their land. The American flag bearer refused to bow before the royal box. The American team captain (who also happened to be Irish) reportedly declared, "This flag dips to no earthly King."

Windsor Castle, seen here in 2006, was chosen as the start of the 1908 marathon event so the royal children could watch the beginning of the race.

In the 400-meter run, the American runner tripped up his British counterpart and went on to win. In the marathon, the Italian won, but only after he was helped, in a state of collapse, across the finish line. It was at these Games, in a serendipitous way, that the official length of the marathon was set. The British royal family asked that the marathon begin at Windsor Castle so the royal children could witness its start. The distance from Windsor Castle to the Olympic stadium was 42,195 meters (or twenty-six miles and 385 yards). So that established its length.

In one notable first, John Taylor, a member of the U.S. medley relay team, became the first African American athlete to win Olympic gold. A graduate of the University of Pennsylvania School of Veterinary Medicine, he had a promising future outside of sports but died suddenly of typhoid fever, at the age of twenty-six, after his return to

The medal from the 1908 Games.

A certificate presented to the silver medalist in featherweight boxing, Charles W. Morris.

the United States. A teammate afterward recalled that he was exemplary as both an athlete and a man.

The Games needed more of Taylor's stamp. Despite their ideal of concord, there was a surprising amount of infighting among the different teams. It was even suggested that the Games be abolished because they fostered more tension than goodwill. That was surely an exaggeration, but it brought their future into question for a time.

In Stockholm four years later, the Games were redeemed. Under the Swedes, they were well financed and organized, emblematic of harmony, and distinguished by judging that was beyond reproach. Indeed, their "mathematical precision" and "formal correctness," as one leading official put it, set a standard for years to come. For these Games, Pierre de Coubertin—ever active in Olympic matters—created two modern pentathlons (an "athletics pentathlon," which combined the broad jump, javelin throw, discus throw, 200-meter dash, and 1,500-meter run, and one that combined riding, running, swimming, fencing, and shooting) as the standard repertoire of Olympic events took shape. An "art competition" (of works based on sports themes) was also introduced, along with the decathlon. The Games began to make headlines, as teams from twenty-six nations took part and a number of new records were set. Moreover, women's events in swimming and diving were introduced, and baseball and glima (Icelandic folk wrestling) were offered as demonstration sports. This allowed sports not yet part of the Olympic program to demonstrate their fitness and appeal.

There were quite a few firsts. One Greco-Roman wrestling bout lasted eleven hours and forty minutes (the world's longest); Swedish marksman Oscar Swahn, at the

The send-off of the American track team to the 1912 Stockholm Games.

At sixty-four, the Swedish shooter Oscar Swahn became the oldest gold medal winner.

age of sixty-four, became the oldest contestant to win a gold medal; and Francisco Lázaro, a Portuguese runner, died of a heart attack in the marathon—the first athlete in the modern Olympics to expire during an event. Another runner, Shizo Kanakuri of Japan, fared almost as badly. Before the Games of 1912, he had set a marathon world record of two hours, thirty-two minutes, and forty-five seconds. During the Olympic race itself, however, he was felled by sunstroke in the blistering heat and was discovered by farmers in a field. Once he recovered, he abruptly returned to Japan. That hurt his international reputation, though in Japan he is still revered as "the father of the marathon."

But the unquestionable star of the Games was Jim Thorpe, the "American Indian giant," who amazed the world with his grace, speed, and strength in the track-and-field events. He won both the pentathlon and the newly created decathlon and defied all doubt as to what he could do. The decathlon was a Herculean challenge in itself, for it combined the 100-meter dash, broad jump, shot put, high jump, 400-meter run, discus throw, 110-meter high hurdles, pole vault, javelin throw, and 1,500-meter run. Thorpe surpassed his nearest competitor, a Swede, by over seven hundred points. The czar of Russia was so excited by this event that he offered to donate a Viking ship as a prize.

Some consider Jim Thorpe the greatest athlete of the twentieth century. Born James Francis Thorpe on May 28, 1888, in a one-room cabin near Prague, Oklahoma, to Hiram Thorpe, a farmer, and Mary James, a Pottawatomie Indian and descendant of a famed warrior chief, Thorpe— who was also known by his tribal name, Wa-Tho-Huk, meaning "bright path"—had a robust childhood on his parents' farm. In those days, there were few opportunities for Native Americans to get a foothold in life, and in 1904 Thorpe enrolled in the Carlisle Indian Industrial School in Carlisle, Pennsylvania, which offered practical training in various trades. The school had an athletic program, and Thorpe played football and took part in track and field. That gave him a chance to demonstrate his athletic potential early on. In 1909 and 1910, he was selected as an all-American (that is, as the member of an honorary team made up of the best amateur athletes in the country), and the following year he made the American Olympic squad. At Stockholm, he overwhelmed all rivals and set records in both the pentathlon and the decathlon that would stand for a long time. When King Gustav V of Sweden presented Thorpe with his gold medals, he grasped Thorpe's hand and said, "Sir, you are the greatest athlete in the world." Thorpe replied simply, "Thanks, King." Many years later, a fellow medalist said that Thorpe "was the greatest athlete who ever lived. . . . What he had was natural ability. There wasn't anything he couldn't do. All he had to see is someone doin' something and he tried it . . . and he'd do it better."

The star of the 1912 Games, Jim Thorpe.

Thorpe at the 1912 Games: throwing the discus (top left), pole-vaulting (top right), and during the long jump (bottom).

The Games made Thorpe an international star. But the following year, it was discovered that he had been paid in the States for two seasons of semi-professional baseball. He hadn't been paid much, but the strict rules governing the amateur status of all athletes technically disqualified him from Olympic sport. So he was stripped of his medals, and his name was deleted from the record books.

Thorpe did his best to move on. Dubbed a professional, he set out to make his name in a professional sports career. He played for a number of baseball and football teams, including the New York Giants, the Boston Braves, and the Cincinnati Reds; organized, coached, and played with a Native American team called the Oorang Indians; became involved in forming the American Professional Football Association (which evolved into the NFL); and otherwise enjoyed a distinguished athletic career.

Yet the loss of his medals was a wound that would not heal. Chief Meyers, a friend and fellow teammate on the New York Giants, recalled, "Jim was very proud of the great things he'd done. A very proud man. . . . Very late one night Jim came in and woke me up. . . . He was crying, and tears were rolling down his cheeks. 'You know, Chief,' he said, 'the King of Sweden gave me those trophies, he gave them to me. But they took them away from me. They're mine, Chief; I won them fair and square.' It broke his heart."

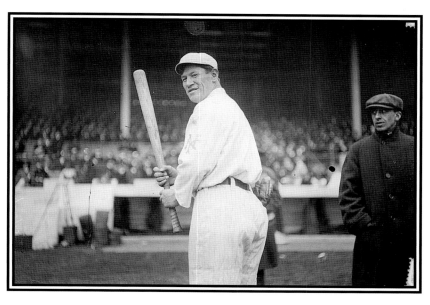

Thorpe in his New York Giants uniform in 1913.

In his deep discouragement, Thorpe drank too much, had an unsettled private life, and when not performing as an athlete, had trouble holding down a job. At one time or another, he worked as an extra in the movies, a park attendant, and a day laborer; hired himself out as a public speaker; and assembled an American Indian song-and-dance troupe, which hit the road as *The Jim Thorpe Show*. In 1945, at the age of fifty-eight, he even joined the merchant marine. By then, he had been all but forgotten. In 1951, however, he was elected to the Football Hall of Fame, and when he died of a heart attack two years later, on March 28, 1953, the *New York Times* ran his obituary on the front page. The *Times* described Thorpe as "a magnificent performer. He had all the strength, speed and coordination of the finest players, plus an incredible stamina. The tragedy of the loss of his Stockholm medals because of thoughtless and unimportant professionalism darkened much of his career and should have been rectified long ago. His memory should be kept for what it deserves—that of the greatest all-around athlete of our time."

In 1982, almost thirty years after his death, Thorpe's medals were finally restored and his name reinscribed in the record books.

The 1912 Stockholm Games had promised to be a springboard for the Olympics to enter a whole new phase. Tremendous excitement therefore began to build ahead of time for the Games of 1916. That prospect was shattered by a horrific war.

If the Games themselves were alive, the Olympic Truce was not.

With Germany arming for war, the International Olympic Committee naively hoped to avert a conflict by awarding the festival to Berlin. But Germany, of course, placed imperial expansion above the ephemeral glamour of the Games.

Archduke Franz Ferdinand of Austria and his family, sometime between 1910 and 1914.

With Europe teetering on the brink, the First World War was triggered by the assassination on June 28, 1914, of Archduke Franz Ferdinand of Austria, the heir to the Austro-Hungarian throne. Several great empires—including the Russian, British, Ottoman, German, and Austro-Hungarian—became involved in an ever-growing conflict as

British soldiers under fire in the trenches in August 1916, during World War I.

competing interests drew different powers together as allies. After Austro-Hungarian troops invaded Serbia, the Russians attacked Germany, and the Germans invaded Belgium, Luxembourg, and France. As the opposing forces entrenched, especially on the eastern and western fronts, the slaughter went on and on with little gain for either side. Over the course of the next few years, more than nine million people were killed. A whole generation of young men was lost. In the end, two main developments determined the outcome. The Russian Empire collapsed in 1917, which allowed the Germans to shift part of their forces from east to west; and the United States entered the war to counter a new German offensive on the western front. At length, Germany was defeated, and on November 11, 1918, the dreadful fighting came to an end.

During the war, the Games had been suspended. When they resumed in 1920, they were awarded to Antwerp in

Returning World War I soldiers parading down Fifth Avenue in New York City in 1919.

At fourteen, Aileen Riggin became the youngest gold medalist at the time when she won the women's springboard diving competition in 1920.

honor of the terrible suffering experienced by the Belgians, whose country had served as one huge battlefield. In a punitive measure, Germany, Austria, and their allies Bulgaria, Hungary, and Turkey were banned. Even so, the Games took place under the shadow of the recent carnage, and embittered veterans could be found on every team. Local enthusiasm was also lacking. The impoverished Belgian population could scarcely afford tickets,

Chamonix, France, was home to the first Winter Games in 1924.

even at a discount, and thousands of schoolchildren had to be brought into the stadium to fill the empty seats. The Games had many hostile moments. The highlight (for the Belgians, at least) was Belgium's face-off with the Czechs in a soccer match. Hundreds of ardent Belgian fans, lacking tickets, dug a tunnel under a perimeter fence and streamed into the stands. The field was lined with soldiers, and the match was fierce. After the Belgians scored on a penalty kick, a Czech was expelled from the game for kicking a Belgian player in the chest. The Czechs walked off the field, and their team was disqualified.

Still, the fact that the Games took place at all was a

kind of triumph. Their athletic highlight was undoubtedly the achievement of Paavo Nurmi of Finland, who paced himself with a stopwatch and took nine medals in track and field. At these Olympics, a number of ceremonial rituals and customs were put in place. These included the hoisting of the host country's flag with a performance of its national anthem, artistic displays of the host country's culture, and the parade of athletes into the stadium in alphabetical order by nation—with Greece, however, coming in first to honor the origins of the Olympics, and the host country last. The medal ceremonies for first, second, and third place were also set. Thereafter, the winners stood on a three-tiered rostrum as their flags were raised and the national anthem of the gold medalist was played.

These Olympics were also the first in which the Olympic oath was pronounced, doves were released to symbolize peace, and the Olympic flag was flown. The Olympic oath read: "In the name of all competitors, I promise that we shall take part in these Olympic Games, respecting and abiding by the rules that govern them, in the true spirit of sportsmanship, for the glory of sport and the honor of our teams." The official Olympic flag, which embodied Coubertin's optimistic hopes for international cooperation, contained five interconnected rings to symbolize the five main inhabited continents linked in friendship. The five colors of the rings—blue, yellow, black, green, and red— were evidently chosen because at least one of them appears in the flag of every country in the world.

Inspired by the success of his banner, Coubertin in the following year came up with the official Olympic motto, which was proposed to him by a friend and Jesuit priest: "Citius, Altius, Fortius" ("Swifter, Higher, Stronger").

The 1924 American boxing team.

That theme of striving was nicely coupled with the Olympic creed: "The most important thing in life is not the triumph but the fight; the essential thing is not to have won, but to have fought well." (In a rather touching example, an Australian rower would take gold despite stopping in midstream to let a mother duck and her ducklings swim safely past his boat.)

By 1920, certain distinctions within a number of contests were also established. A sport was distinguished from a discipline, a discipline being a division of a sport. For example, the sport of wrestling was said to comprise two disciplines: Greco-Roman and freestyle. Over the years, different sports and disciplines would come and go, but the mainstays remained. Meanwhile, in the Games of 1920, twenty-nine nations participated in thirty disciplines and twenty-eight sports. The Games also featured a week of winter competitions, with figure skating (first introduced in the summer of 1908) and ice hockey making their Olympic debut as winter sports.

The Olympic Movement soldiered on. More and more

countries took part with each Games (forty-four in Paris in 1924; about fifty in Amsterdam in 1928). All along, the Summer Olympics had provided little opportunity for the display of winter sports. Obviously, summer weather made them impractical. The Winter Olympics were therefore created as a separate event to feature snow and ice sports that were impossible to hold during the summer months. A winter sports week (it was actually eleven days) was held in 1924 at the foot of Mont Blanc in Chamonix, France, from January 25 to February 5—the first Winter Olympic Games.

Athletes from sixteen nations competed in eleven events, including bobsleigh, ski jumping, Nordic combined (ski jumping and cross-country skiing), curling, figure skating, ice hockey, speed skating, and military patrol. Military patrol (a combination of cross-country skiing and shooting at targets) was offered as a demonstration sport. Following this precedent, the Winter Olympics would continue to be held every four years, in the same year as the Summer Games, until 1992, when the Summer and Winter Games began to alternate every two years.

In 1924, the Summer Olympics were once more held in Paris. Athletes from forty-four nations competed in thirty-two events (including rope climbing). Basque pelota was a demonstration sport, along with canoeing, jeu de paume, la canne (stick fighting), savate (kickboxing), and volleyball. Ireland debuted at the Games as an independent nation. In one startling outcome, the winner in the rifle event prevailed after being accidentally shot in the middle of the match.

The 1924 Games also effectively marked Pierre de Coubertin's farewell. He had been the moving force behind the Olympics from the outset and contributed more to the Games than any other man. Perhaps the satisfaction he gained from his achievements provided some compensation for the tragedies that marked his private life. His son suffered brain damage, his daughter was emotionally disturbed, and his two nephews (whom he cherished as his own children) had both been killed in World War I.

Although the 1924 Summer Olympics produced few notable displays of athletic skill, two Americans especially excelled. Harold Osborn won gold medals and set Olympic records in both the high jump and the decathlon, and Johnny Weissmuller won three gold medals in swimming and a bronze in water polo.

Johnny Weissmuller at an Olympic swim meet on July 28, 1924.

Weissmuller had quite a career. In sports, he would eventually win five Olympic gold medals and fifty-two U.S. national championships and set sixty-seven world records. In fact, he never lost a race. Outside of sports, he played Tarzan, with his distinctive ululating, yodeling yell, in twelve films.

An Austro-Hungarian immigrant, Weissmuller had come to America with his parents when he was a child. At the age of nine, he contracted polio, which might have crippled him, but at the behest of his doctor, he tried swimming to strengthen his limbs. That worked, and swimming became the thing he loved most. He dropped out of high school and worked as a lifeguard at a Lake Michigan beach, then as a bellboy at the Illinois Athletic Club. There he was allowed to use the pool during off-hours, and one day he caught the eye of a swimming coach. The coach worked with him day and night, and in August 1921 Weissmuller won the national championships in the 50-yard and 220-yard distance races at the age of seventeen. On July 9, 1922, he broke the world record in the 100-meter freestyle. He was invited to join the United States Olympic team, and in order to make the squad he lied about his foreign birth.

At the 1924 Olympics, he won the 100-meter freestyle for the gold. Eight years later, in 1932, Weissmuller became an overnight international sensation when he played Tarzan in *Tarzan the Ape Man,* the first and most famous of his tremendously popular films.

His celebrity, not incidentally, cut across ideological lines. During the Communist revolution under Fidel Castro in 1958, Weissmuller happened to be in a golf tournament in Cuba. Suddenly a band of revolutionaries surrounded his golf cart. Weissmuller got out and gave his trademark Tarzan yell. The rebels recognized it at once, put down their arms, and exclaimed, "Tarzan, Tarzan, welcome to Cuba!" When he died, a recording of his yell was played in eerie tribute as his body was placed in its grave.

The second Winter Olympics was held in mid-February in St. Moritz, Switzerland, in 1928, and the Summer

Olympics that year were in the Netherlands, in Amsterdam. Most notably, women's track and field and gymnastics made their debut. Halina Konopacka of Poland won the discus throw and became the first female Olympic champion in track and field, Johnny Weissmuller again proved the swimming star, India took its first-ever gold medal in field hockey, Germany returned to the Games (and finished second in the medal count), and the Dutch gymnast Helena Nordheim won gold to emerge as a new international star. To spur on the American team, General Douglas MacArthur, then head of the American Olympic Committee, did his utmost to link sports with national pride. "Nothing is more synonymous of our national success," he declared, "than is our national success in athletics."

The Olympic Games were now established. No one doubted they were here to stay. Even the Great Depression couldn't sink them. Nevertheless, when the 1932 Winter Olympics were held in Lake Placid, New York, only seventeen nations sent athletes to compete, and the festival was pervaded by a sense of gloom. The economic crisis had taken hold worldwide. When the Summer Olympics were held in 1932 in Los Angeles, many nations

A panoramic view of Los Angeles Memorial Coliseum as the athletes take the Olympic oath on the opening day of the 1932 Summer Games.

and athletes could not afford to compete, although a huge new coliseum was built for the occasion and a handsome Olympic Village set up on a rolling tract of land. President Herbert Hoover—facing imminent defeat by Franklin D. Roosevelt in the upcoming presidential election—also did not attend, though in the past every host country had had its head of state, or a representative, present to preside. (After all, every Olympics, no matter how poorly managed, provided a chance for the host country to advertise itself.)

In some sports, the competition was also thin. For example, only three nations competed in field hockey. In other curious standouts, a Polish American woman by the name of Stanisława Walasiewicz, who turned out to be a hermaphrodite, won five gold medals in track and field, and Japan won its only gold medal ever in the equestrian event. The winner, Takeichi Nishi, became a friend of several Hollywood stars (including Douglas Fairbanks and Mary Pickford) but was said to be closest of all to his beloved horse, Uranus, which he had bought in Italy a few years before. Nishi would later serve as a tank unit commander in the Japanese Imperial Army and would be killed in action by Allied forces on the island of Iwo Jima in World War II.

CHAPTER SIX

Athletic Politics

The next round of Games was slated for Berlin. When the decision was made to bring them there, the Nazis had not yet come to power. But by 1932, the world had changed. Japan had abandoned the League of Nations (an international organization of states founded at the end of World War I to prevent another global conflict), Italy had invaded Ethiopia, the French government was crumbling, Adolf Hitler had begun to talk about world domination, and Spain was on the verge of civil war.

Europe had once more become an armed camp.

Hitler was a pathological tyrant who had once been a semi-homeless vagrant. His confused view of the world fostered an extreme political movement, which, by a series of unhappy accidents, found itself at the forefront of German life. Hitler, as the head of the Nazi Party, became chancellor of the German state. He believed in racial purity and white supremacy, and he ascribed every social ill to the Jews. He also imagined himself as the founder of a worldwide German empire, which he called the Third Reich. It was his deluded prediction that it would last a thousand years. Hitler's sinister political philosophy was a mix of capitalism, socialism, nationalism, and racism.

Adolf Hitler (standing in car) greeting the crowd with the Nazi salute in Nuremberg, Germany, in 1935.

By exploiting the discontent of the German people in the post–World War I years, he bent the nation to his will. By 1936, he had also forged an unholy alliance of aggression with Italy and Japan. Together these three states were known as the Axis powers.

Then came the Olympic Games.

The Winter and Summer Olympics of 1936 were viewed as bonanza opportunities for propaganda by the new Nazi regime. The Winter Olympics were held in the market town of Garmisch-Partenkirchen in Bavaria and organized on behalf of the sports office of the Third Reich by Karl Ritter von Halt. Von Halt had been a track-

and-field athlete who had competed in the 1912 Stockholm Olympics. He had not been a star—he had finished twenty-second in the javelin throw competition, fourteenth in the shot put, and ninth in the decathlon—but he was a genuine sports enthusiast. The Summer Games were held in Berlin. Twenty-eight nations sent athletes to the Winter Games, forty-nine to the Summer Games. Six nations made their first official Olympic appearance: Afghanistan, Bermuda, Bolivia, Costa Rica, Liechtenstein, and Peru. The German teams did well in the Winter Games, as two German athletes won gold medals in the new Alpine skiing event, which combined a skier's results in both the downhill and slalom (zigzagging through poles). Norway's Sonja Henie won her third consecutive gold medal in women's figure skating, and Norway won overall with a total of seven gold medals, five silver, and three bronze.

Hitler himself wasn't particularly enthusiastic about the Olympics. After all, he was a nationalist, and the

Berlin during the 1936 Summer Olympics.

Hitler's minister of propaganda, Joseph Goebbels, believed that Olympic sport would endow the German people with the "fighting spirit." (c. July 1932)

Games were a big international event. But he decided to use them to portray himself in a positive, peace-loving light. "The sportive, knightly battle awakens the best human characteristics," he declared. "It doesn't separate, but unites the combatants in understanding and respect. It also helps to connect the countries in the spirit of peace. That's why the Olympic Flame should never die." So he said in public. But Joseph Goebbels, his alter ego and minister of propaganda, harped in private on a rather different theme: "German sport has only one task: to strengthen the character of the German people, imbuing it with the fighting spirit and steadfast camaraderie necessary in the struggle for its existence." Indeed, not unlike some ancient Greeks, a number of German sports officials viewed athletics as a form of disciplined military training rather than wholesome exercise or sport. At the same time, they believed that sports were, as he put it, a "way to weed out the weak, Jewish, and other undesirables."

The German mastermind of the Summer Games was Carl Diem, secretary-general of the organizing committee. Together with his partner, Theodor Lewald, he had been an Olympic enthusiast and disciple of Coubertin. Nevertheless, both had to watch their own backs. Diem's wife was Jewish. Lewald had Jewish blood.

Meanwhile, the United States had considered boycotting the Games on the grounds that its participation might be viewed as support for the Nazi regime. However, others argued that the Olympic Games should not be politicized. Avery Brundage, then president of the American Olympic Association (and subsequently president of the International Olympic Committee from 1952 to 1972), opposed the boycott, stating, "The very foundation of the modern Olympic revival will be undermined if individual countries are allowed to restrict participation by reason of class, creed, or race." In principle, that sounded good. But Brundage also reportedly feared that there was a "Jewish-Communist conspiracy" against the United States taking part.

At the same time, the Nazis put on a pretend show of good faith by including Helene Mayer, a blacklisted Jewish athlete and world-class fencer, on their own roster. On the face of it, they could hardly fail to gain. Mayer had first made her mark as all-German champion at the age of thirteen. In subsequent years, she had bested almost all her rivals, both in Germany and abroad. (In the upcoming Games, she would star once more and take a silver medal in her sport.)

However, the American Olympic Association remained skeptical, and a movement to boycott the Berlin Games began to gather steam. Diem's old friend Avery Brundage was dispatched to Berlin to assess the situation, and Diem convinced Brundage that Jews were being allowed to compete. Brundage was eager to be won over and returned to America to persuade his colleagues to accept the invitation to participate.

He met resistance. The Amateur Athletic Union, for example, held that by agreeing to compete in the Games, Americans would be lending "moral and financial support to the Nazi regime, which is opposed to all that Americans hold dearest." Various religious, political, and civic leaders also objected to participation, and the Spanish government, led by the newly elected and progressive Popular Front, planned to boycott the Games and organize a People's Olympiad as a parallel event in Barcelona, Spain.

For its own reasons, on the other hand, the black community wanted the Games to go on. Since black American athletes were expected to do well, it was thought that "black victories would undermine Nazi views of Aryan supremacy and spark renewed African American pride."

Meanwhile, throughout Germany, Jewish athletes were "banned from city playgrounds and sports facilities, gymnastic organizations, physical education programs, [and] public swimming pools."

The Nazis went all out to seduce their critics. They built a huge 325-acre sports complex about five miles west of Berlin, with a gigantic stadium of natural stone that could seat 110,000.

The Germans also created a model 130-acre Olympic Village "laid out in the shape of a map of Germany and containing 140 buildings including a post office and bank. Each of the athletes' houses contained thirteen bedrooms, with two athletes per room. Two stewards, who spoke the athletes' native language, were always on duty in each house, and training facilities in the village included a 400-meter oval track and a full-size indoor swimming pool." The village, constructed by the German army, "was the finest housing ever provided to Olympic athletes up to that time."

Berlin was also spruced up. Disgraceful emblems of Nazi intolerance, such as "Jews Not Welcome" signs, were taken down, and Nazi storm troopers "were ordered to refrain from any actions against Jews." Anyone deemed disreputable or a nuisance (such as Gypsies, classed as vagrants), as well as derelicts and the homeless, was picked up in a general dragnet and interned.

Meanwhile, on a visit to Greece for an Olympic conference in 1934, Diem and Lewald had come up with the idea of a torch relay from Greece to Berlin. It was at the Berlin Games that the torch relay (now an Olympic trademark) made its debut. At noon on July 20, 1936, twelve days before the start of the Games, a "Greek 'high priestess' and fourteen girls wearing classical robes gathered in the ancient stadium of Olympia and used parabolic mirrors to focus the sun's rays on a wand until it burst into

The lighting of the torch before the relay at the ancient stadium in Olympia.

flame." The flame, igniting a torch, was then carried by 3,075 relay runners to Berlin from Greece.

On Saturday, August 1, 1936, the Games opened in the Olympic Stadium to a capacity crowd. More than five thousand athletes from fifty-one nations marched in. But almost at once, a problem arose. The so-called Olympic salute—with the right arm held out sideways from the shoulder—closely resembled the Nazi salute. Should athletes give the Nazi salute to Hitler as they passed by his reviewing stand? If they gave the Olympic salute, who would know? The British and Americans gave neither. The Americans also declined to dip their flag while passing by the reviewing stand.

After Hitler proclaimed the Games open, an Olympic hymn, reluctantly written by the German composer Richard Strauss (who hated sports), was sung, followed by the arrival of the Olympic torch.

The arrival of the Olympic torch at the Berlin stadium.

Although the U.S. Olympic team included eighteen African Americans and five Jews, Jewish athletes from some other countries chose in protest not to attend.

Sporting competitions began the next day, Sunday, August 2, with the track-and-field events. Hitler imagined the Games would demonstrate the Nazi creed of Aryan superiority (at least in the realm of sports), but his dreams were shattered when four black American athletes, including the great Jesse Owens from Ohio State University, won six events. Owens won four gold medals: one each in the 100-meter and 200-meter races, one in the long jump, and one as part of the 4,000-meter relay team.

Born James Cleveland Owens in Oakville, Alabama, on September 12, 1913, Owens moved with his family to Cleveland, Ohio, at the age of nine as part of the Great Migration of African Americans from the segregated South. When his new teacher asked his name to enter in her roll book, he said "J.C." in a thick southern drawl. She thought he said "Jesse," and the name stuck.

Early on, Owens became interested in track and field and was luckily encouraged by his junior high school coach. Like Jim Thorpe, he was a natural, and a few years later, at East Technical High School in Cleveland, he astonished officials by equaling the world record of 9.4 seconds in the 100-yard dash.

Owens went on to Ohio State University, where he was known as the Buckeye Bullet. He won eight individual National Collegiate Athletic Association championships, and on May 25, 1935, at the Big Ten meet in Ann Arbor, Michigan, he set three world records—in the long jump, the 220-yard sprint, and the 220-yard low hurdles—and tied a fourth in the 100-yard dash.

Jesse Owens at the start of his record-breaking 200-meter dash in 1936.

He once explained his success in the simplest terms: "I let my feet spend as little time on the ground as possible. From the air, fast down, and from the ground, fast up." There was no question that Owens would be selected for the 1936 Olympic team. He was singled out as a star even before the Games began. No sooner had he settled into his room in the Olympic Village than he was visited by Adi

Dassler, the future founder of the Adidas athletic-shoe company, who persuaded him to use Dassler shoes (instead of Keds sneakers) in his events. Owens thereby became the first black American athlete to be hired as the official sponsor of commercial goods.

Basketball and handball made their debut at the Olympics (both, incidentally, as outdoor sports), and baseball and gliding were offered as demonstration sports. The basketball final between Canada and the United States was played outdoors on a dirt court in driving rain. Because of the quagmire, the teams could not dribble, so the score was incredibly low—the United States prevailing 19–8. Americans also won gold in the 800-meter race, the decathlon, and the rowing contest. In the marathon, two Korean athletes won medals—Sohn Kee-chung (gold) and Nam Sung-yong (bronze)—running for Japan and under Japanese names (since Japan had annexed Korea in 1910). British India once more took gold in the field hockey event, defeating Germany 8–1, and the Egyptian weight lifter Khadr El Touni defeated two German world champions.

Here and there the rules were bent on Germany's behalf. In the cycling match sprint finals, for example, the German Toni Merkens fouled Arie van Vliet of the Netherlands. But instead of being disqualified, Merkens was fined one hundred marks and allowed to keep the gold. Political grandstanding of one sort or another also marred the Games. The fact that Italy's soccer team proved dominant was hyped by supporters of Benito Mussolini to glorify his Fascist regime. Peru's soccer win over Austria, on the other hand, was discounted on a disputed technicality (mainly at Hitler's behest).

Dora Ratjen replaced a female Jewish high jumper on the German team but was later revealed to be a man.

Meanwhile, in the interest of preserving the racial purity of their team, the Germans were willing to savage their own. Gretel Bergmann, for example, despite equaling a national record in the high jump a month before the Games, had been excluded from the team because she was Jewish. She was replaced by high jumper Dora Ratjen, who was later revealed to be a man. Behind the scenes, Avery Brundage, now the American Olympic Association president, evidently played an unsavory role. In unspoken collusion with Nazi sentiment, he yanked two Jewish American sprinters, Sam Stoller and Marty Glickman, from the relay team on the day of the competition so as not to enrage Hitler, it is said, "by having two Jews win gold."

Brundage's treatment of the two Jewish American athletes was an obvious disgrace. As a sprinter and long jumper, Sam Stoller was the only real rival to Jesse Owens, and for years they had competed against each other in high school and college meets. The two became good friends. Stoller had had his own moment in the sun when he tied the world record in the 60-yard dash at the Big Ten championships in March 1936. He had also qualified, along with Marty Glickman and their fellow athlete Foy Draper, for the Olympic 4-by-100-meter relay team.

On the morning that the 4-by-100-meter relay competition was to begin, however, the U.S. track coach, Lawson Robertson, and his assistant, Dean Cromwell, announced that Stoller and Glickman would be replaced by Owens and Ralph Metcalfe, a fellow runner, because "the Germans were saving their best sprinters, hiding them, to upset the American team." Glickman found that preposterous and objected: "Coach, you can't hide world-class sprinters." Owens also objected, speaking up on behalf of Glickman and Stoller: "Coach, I've won my three gold medals. I'm tired. I've had it. Let Marty and Sam run, they deserve it." But Dean Cromwell snapped, "You'll do as you're told." As it turned out, the American team won, and did so with a new world-record time. But most observers thought the Americans would have won anyway. Germany's "hidden sprinters" failed to materialize.

Brundage and the two track coaches later denied that prejudice had anything to do with their actions and said that they only wanted to put the best men in the race. But four or five days earlier, in a trial contest to determine the running order, Stoller had finished first, Glickman second, and Foy Draper third. Stoller and Glickman were also more experienced in passing the baton—an important feature of the race. Even so, some sports historians remain convinced that Brundage meant well and that, in his heart of hearts, he was a sincere apostle of the Olympic ideals.

Despite the politically charged atmosphere of the Berlin Games, Owens was adored by the German public. Germans sought his autograph, and he was cheered by the stadium crowd. (Goebbels grumbled, "If America didn't have her black auxiliaries, where would she be in the Olympic Games.") Owens also began a long-term friendship with his German rival Carl Ludwig "Luz" Long. At the time, Long held the European record in the long jump and was eager to compete against Owens in that event. Owens, however, almost failed to qualify after two false starts. Long then gave him some helpful advice. He went over and suggested Owens try to jump from a spot behind the takeoff board. Since Owens often made jumps beyond the minimum needed to advance, Long

Luz Long recording a 7.87-meter long jump at the Berlin Games.

rightly figured he would still make the grade. Owens heeded Long's advice, qualified, and won. Long took the silver—and was the first to congratulate Owens, despite the fact that Hitler was looking down on them from the stands. Then Long walked arm in arm with Owens to the dressing room.

Long went on to study law at the University of Leipzig and worked as a lawyer in Hamburg before the Second World War broke out. Like most young Germans, he enlisted in the German army, but he did not survive the war. He was fatally wounded in the Allied invasion of Sicily in 1943.

Naoto Tajima, Jesse Owens, and Luz Long (from left to right) at the long jump medal ceremony.

Though Jesse Owens was black (and therefore despised by the Nazis as non-Aryan), he could move about Berlin freely, stay in the same hotels as whites, use public transportation, and enter restaurants and other public facilities without hindrance. By contrast, he faced segregation, restriction of movement, and other indignities at home in the United States. The irony of this was not lost on him. When it was reported that Hitler had deliberately avoided acknowledging Owens's victories and had refused to shake his hand, Owens said that wasn't true. "When I passed the chancellor, he arose, waved his hand at me, and I waved back at him"; whereas (he later recalled), after a New York City ticker-tape parade on Fifth Avenue, he had to take the freight elevator at the Waldorf-Astoria to the room where he was the honored guest. "Hitler didn't snub me," Owens said. "It was our president [FDR] who snubbed me. The president didn't even send me a telegram." That was certainly a grievous oversight on FDR's part.

Despite Hitler's brief acknowledgment of Owens, his contempt for those he deemed inferior surfaced in private readily enough. Albert Speer, Hitler's architect and later his war armaments minister, wrote in his memoirs, *Inside the Third Reich*: "Each of the German victories—and there were a surprising number of these—made him happy, but he was highly annoyed by the series of triumphs by the marvelous colored American runner, Jesse Owens. People whose antecedents came from the jungle were primitive, Hitler said with a shrug, their physiques were stronger than those of civilized whites. They represented unfair competition and hence must be excluded from future games. Hitler was also jolted by the jubilation of the

Berliners when the French team filed solemnly into the Olympic Stadium. . . . If I am correctly interpreting Hitler's expression at the time, he was more disturbed than pleased by the Berliners' cheers."

Notwithstanding his anger at the U.S. government, Owens understood, of course, what a bigot Hitler was. "It took a lot of courage for [Luz Long] to befriend me in front of Hitler," he recalled. "You can melt down all the medals and cups I have and they wouldn't be a plating on the twenty-four-karat friendship I felt for Luz Long at that moment."

Epilogue

The Berlin Games concluded on Sunday, August 16, 1936, with Germany as the overall victor, capturing eighty-nine medals. The Americans came in second with fifty-six. Internationally, interest in the Games was intense. Within Germany, the Games were the first to be televised live to special viewing rooms throughout Potsdam and Berlin. About 162,000 Germans watched the Games on twenty-five large screens. This was an exciting development and helped establish the use of television as an effective marketing tool to promote Olympic sports.

Leni Riefenstahl, the documentarian who captured the Games on film, shaking hands with Adolf Hitler. (c. 1934)

A remarkable record of their highlights was captured by Leni Riefenstahl in her film *Olympia*, the greatest sports documentary ever made. Though Riefenstahl was later stigmatized as a Nazi propagandist—with reason, based on her film *Triumph of the Will*—in *Olympia* she was really interested in two things: the power of spectacle and the beauty of the human form. Her film opened with idealized images from ancient Greek sport that morphed into German athletes. But the stars of her film were not Germans; they were whoever excelled. For that reason, if the film had a star, it was Jesse Owens, to whom she devoted a good deal of time. There was also admiring footage of many other non-Germans. But aside from that, it is an important film in the history of moviemaking, for Riefenstahl invented all kinds of new ways to use the camera lens.

Essentially, she turned the stadium in Berlin into a Hollywood-style motion-picture studio. For example, she developed traveling shots (with her crew shooting on roller skates as well as from multiple angles), pioneered the use of the telephoto lens to create the impression of compactness, and cut her film in time to music to give it the quality of a dance. She built a track with a catapult so that the camera could move alongside sprinters, dug a camera pit (like a foxhole) for the pole vault and high jump so athletes could be filmed against the sky, developed a special 600mm telephoto lens for close-ups, and every day sent up a balloon with a tiny 5mm camera to get an overall aerial view. Everything was carefully choreographed. Little, if anything, was left to chance. Certain dramatic scenes in the film were taken from training footage and spliced into the final version. In scene after scene, she demonstrated a keen eye and a superb ability to compose shots. For the marathon, she used cinematic techniques to capture the grueling ordeal of the runners in all their sweat and pain. Instead of filming the race stride by stride, she tried to show the feelings and mental state of the runners with close-ups. With a skillful use of music, too, she managed to capture both their exhaustion and their will to go on. And all this was mixed in with strong crowd-reaction shots.

Before Riefenstahl's film, diving events had always been shown in a single shot—the diver plunging into the pool. Riefenstahl, however, shot each dive three ways: from above, from below (beneath the water), and opposite (using slow motion). The underwater camera changed speed and focus as the dive unfolded, and different tempos were used for different dives to heighten

A sampling of stills from Leni Riefenstahl's film Olympia.

some effects. Sometimes she even showed the sequences backward, with the divers reversing through the air, to enhance the feeling of movement. In combination, these techniques gave the athletes a beautiful winged, acrobatic quality never before achieved. It also transformed their sometimes contorted gyrations into elegant images of nimbleness and strength.

In the making of *Olympia,* Riefenstahl had thirty-three camera operators at her disposal and shot over a million feet—or 250 miles—of film. It took her eighteen months to edit it all down to a manageable and coherent length (four hours), and beginning in April 1938, she released it in two parts. Curiously enough, politics had no effect on its success. The film was a hit worldwide, drew huge crowds in France and other countries hostile to the rise of German power, and won many awards. Her film also led to greater interest in sports photography and inspired new efforts to record and broadcast sports events. In 1948, the BBC would reach over half a million people within a fifty-mile radius of London with its live television coverage. And in 1960, at the Winter Games held in Squaw Valley, California, even more would view Olympic competitions broadcast live on American TV.

In the aftermath of the 1936 Games, wars and rumors of wars disrupted the planning of future Olympics. Japan was supposed to host the 1940 Winter Games but declined to do so. Instead, it invaded China. The International Olympic Committee looked to Germany to repeat its hospitality, but Germany said no. Instead, it invaded Poland. Finland stepped forward to host the Games but was invaded by Soviet troops. So the 1940 Games were scrapped. Oddly enough, Fascist Italy was then singled out as the proper host for the next round. However, by the time 1944 arrived, the Allies had overrun Italy and were bombarding hundreds of sites where Italian and German forces were entrenched.

All this was due to the Second World War, which lasted from 1939 to 1945 and involved most of the world's nations, several continents, and all of the great powers. It began with the German invasion of Poland on September 1, 1939. After Britain and France declared war on Germany two days later, the fighting spread. Eventually, the war was fought out in North Africa, on the high seas, in Asia, and on two main European fronts. Germany faced the Soviet Union in the east, France and Britain in the west. The United States unofficially entered the war on behalf of Britain in 1940 and openly in December 1941 after the Japanese attacked Pearl Harbor in Hawaii, where the U.S. Pacific fleet was moored. The Axis powers were at first triumphant. But in 1942, the tide of the war began to turn. It ended in Europe with the fall of Berlin to Soviet troops and the unconditional surrender of Germany on May 8, 1945. By that time, carpet bombing had reduced Germany to rubble, and the Japanese were on the verge of defeat. Still, they fought on, and an Allied invasion of Japan loomed. After two devastating nuclear attacks

Czechoslovakian locals express mixed reactions as they greet German troops with the Nazi salute. (c. October 1938)

on Hiroshima and Nagasaki by the United States—the first and only time nuclear weapons have been used— Japan formally surrendered on September 2, 1945.

Many crimes were committed during the war, but the worst of them was the Holocaust. This was a diabolical attempt by the Nazis to kill every single Jew in Europe. In the end, six million Jews were systematically killed. Quite a few were Jewish Olympic athletes. One was Helena Nordheim, the Dutch gymnast who had won the gold medal at the 1928 Summer Olympics in her native Amsterdam. She was killed with her husband and ten-year-old daughter in 1943 in Poland at the Sobibor extermination camp. Another was Alfred Flatow, who had won the

The shoes of just some of the Jewish victims at the concentration camp in Auschwitz, Poland.

individual and team parallel bars competitions for Germany and placed second on the horizontal bar at the 1896 Athens Olympics. At the age of seventy-three, Flatow was deported from Berlin to the Theresienstadt ghetto, forty miles from Prague, where he was starved to death. Still another was Ilja Szrajbman, the national champion for Poland in the men's 200-meter freestyle swim event. He competed in the 1936 Berlin Games only to perish in the Warsaw ghetto in 1943.

The sad list is a long one. It would be too much to name them all.

In a different kind of postscript to the war, the subsequent careers of some other Olympic figures deserve to be singled out. Despite being classified as a "white Jew" (or impure Aryan), Carl Diem, the mastermind of the Berlin Games, remained loyal throughout to the Third Reich. In March 1945, as the Red Army was closing in on Berlin, Diem exhorted thousands of teenage members of the Hitler Youth movement to defend the city to the death. It was an act of criminal folly on his part and led to a grotesque slaughter of the young. Nevertheless, Diem's reputation was rehabilitated after the war; he once more became a respected national figure and had a sports institute named after him, which was run by his wife.

Then there was Sonja Henie, the Norwegian skater, whom Hitler adored. As a figure skater, Henie had a stellar career. In fact, she won more Olympic and world titles than any other female figure skater in history. She was much in demand as a performer at exhibitions in both Europe and America, where her short skirts, sparkling manner, and theatrical style helped make figure skating into the glamorous Olympic sport it remains to this day.

But her politics shadowed her career. She admired Hitler, had met with him socially, and treasured an inscribed photograph he gave her as a memento. She used her ties with the Nazi regime to protect her family's assets during the German occupation of her native land.

Sonja Henie on the ice in January 1931.

As for Jesse Owens, fortune failed to follow fame. He fell on hard times, but after President Dwight D. Eisenhower made him a U.S. goodwill ambassador in 1955, he traveled the world and found himself in demand as an inspirational speaker before corporate groups. In 1976, he received the Presidential Medal of Freedom, and in 1990 he was posthumously awarded the Congressional Gold Medal—a fitting salute to his glorious career.

Meanwhile, the Olympics made a comeback, though at first on a reduced scale. Europe was exhausted, the austerities that followed the war (food and gas rationing, for example) were still being felt, and spectator interest in the 1948 Games, held in London, lagged. Competing athletes had to borrow each other's equipment, and instead of taking up residence in an Olympic Village, athletes were housed that summer at military installations like airplane hangars and in university dorms. A dog track at Wembley Stadium served as a running track for hurdles and sprints; a defrosted ice rink became a swimming pool. Unable to afford floodlights for the equestrian events, Olympic officials asked car owners to illuminate the track with the headlights of their cars.

Some changes in the general Olympic program were also made. All along, one of the more unusual features of the modern Olympics had been an art competition, begun in 1912. The visual arts (drawing, painting, etching, engraving, and architectural design) tended to dominate, but literature was included, too. As in the athletic competitions, gold, silver, and bronze medals were given out.

This drawing by Jean Jacoby, titled Rugby, *was the gold-medal winner in the 1928 Olympic art competition.*

But since there were no objective standards for the judges to apply—and no clear line between amateur and professional artists—the competition was dropped after 1948.

As one Olympic tradition came to an end, another was born. Ludwig Guttmann of England's Stoke Mandeville Hospital founded the "parallel Olympics" (now called the Paralympics) to honor veterans with spinal cord injuries from the war. In subsequent years, the doctor's idea of establishing an Olympics for the handicapped gained acceptance, and since 1960 the Paralympics have been held in every Olympic year.

Despite the Olympic creed of goodwill and cooperation, real peace was fleeting, and international conflict continued to disrupt the Games from time to time. From the 1950s on, the postwar Olympics were marked by the tensions of the new Cold War. The face-off in various competitions between the United States and the Soviet Union heightened dramatic interest, but it also turned the competitions into surrogate sparring matches between the two great powers and their allies.

Subsequent Games were marred not only by political strife and scandal but even by violence. Black American athletes raised their fists in protest against racial discrimination in the United States in 1968. On September 5, 1972, Arab terrorists attacked the Israeli quarters in the Olympic Village and made a bloodbath of the Munich Games, murdering eleven Israeli athletes. South African apartheid prompted a pan-African boycott in 1976. In 1980, the United States refused to attend the Moscow Olympics after the Soviets invaded Afghanistan. Four years later, when the Games returned to Los Angeles, the Russians responded in kind. From 1988 on, there were doping scandals related to the use of performance-enhancing steroids. And as late as 1999, the Games were tarred by corruption when it was found that key officials of the organizing committee for the Salt Lake City Winter Olympics had obtained the Games through bribery.

Yet it is worth remembering that the ancient Games had their share of troubles, too. There is nothing new under the sun. And through it all—even after professionals largely replaced amateurs in the competition (after 1988) and some landed lucrative endorsement deals—stupendous athletic feats have continued to sustain the dignity of the Olympics and keep their ideals alive.

An ancient Greek philosopher (and fan of the Games) once said that all wise men are friends even if they don't know each other. With equal justice, it may be said that all those who have managed to surpass themselves to achieve athletic greatness in Olympic history—from Theagenes of Thasos to Jesse Owens to Nadia Comaneci—belong to the same immortal team.

Appendix

OLYMPIC MEDAL RECORDS, 1896 TO 1948

1896 OLYMPICS

Rank	Nation	Gold	Silver	Bronze	Total
1	United States	11	7	2	20
2	Greece (host nation)	10	17	19	46
3	Germany	6	5	2	13
4	France	5	4	2	11
5	Great Britain	2	3	2	7
6	Hungary	2	1	3	6
7	Austria	2	1	2	5
8	Australia	2	0	0	2
9	Denmark	1	2	3	6
10	Switzerland	1	2	0	3

1900 OLYMPICS

Rank	Nation	Gold	Silver	Bronze	Total
1	France (host nation)	26	41	34	101
2	United States	19	14	14	47
3	Great Britain	15	6	9	30
4	Mixed team	6	3	3	12
5	Switzerland	6	2	1	9
6	Belgium	5	5	5	15
7	Germany	4	2	2	8
8	Italy	2	2	0	4
9	Australia	2	0	3	5
10	Denmark	1	3	2	6

1904 Olympics

Rank	Nation	Gold	Silver	Bronze	Total
1	United States (host nation)	78	82	79	239
2	Germany	4	4	5	13
3	Cuba	4	2	3	9
4	Canada	4	1	1	6
5	Hungary	2	1	1	4
6 {	Great Britain	1	1	0	2
	Mixed team	1	1	0	2
7 {	Greece	1	0	1	2
	Switzerland	1	0	1	2
8	France	0	0	0	0

1908 Olympics

Rank	Nation	Gold	Silver	Bronze	Total
1	Great Britain (host nation)	56	51	39	146
2	United States	23	12	12	47
3	Sweden	8	6	11	25
4	France	5	5	9	19
5	Germany	3	5	5	13
6	Hungary	3	4	2	9
7	Canada	3	3	10	16
8	Norway	2	3	3	8
9	Italy	2	2	0	4
10	Belgium	1	5	2	8

1912 Olympics

Rank	Nation	Gold	Silver	Bronze	Total
1	United States	25	19	19	63
2	Sweden (host nation)	24	24	17	65
3	Great Britain	10	15	16	41
4	Finland	9	8	9	26
5	France	7	4	3	14

6	Germany	5	13	7	25
7	South Africa	4	2	0	6
8	Norway	4	1	4	9
9 {	Canada	3	2	3	8
	Hungary	3	2	3	8

1920 OLYMPICS

Rank	Nation	Gold	Silver	Bronze	Total
1	United States	41	27	27	95
2	Sweden	19	20	25	64
3	Great Britain	15	15	13	43
4	Finland	15	10	9	34
5	Belgium (host nation)	14	11	11	36
6	Norway	13	9	9	31
7	Italy	13	5	5	23
8	France	9	19	13	41
9	Netherlands	4	2	5	11
10	Denmark	3	9	1	13

1924 WINTER OLYMPICS

Rank	Nation	Gold	Silver	Bronze	Total
1	Norway	4	7	6	17
2	Finland	4	4	3	11
3	Austria	2	1	0	3
4	Switzerland	2	0	1	3
5	United States	1	2	1	4
6	Great Britain	1	1	2	4
7	Sweden	1	1	0	2
8	Canada	1	0	0	1
9	France (host nation)	0	0	3	3
10	Belgium	0	0	1	1

1924 Summer Olympics

Rank	Nation	Gold	Silver	Bronze	Total
1	United States	45	27	27	99
2	Finland	14	13	10	37
3	France (host nation)	13	15	10	38
4	Great Britain	9	13	12	34
5	Italy	8	3	5	16
6	Switzerland	7	8	10	25
7	Norway	5	2	3	10
8	Sweden	4	13	12	29
9	Netherlands	4	1	5	10
10	Belgium	3	7	3	13

1928 Winter Olympics

Rank	Nation	Gold	Silver	Bronze	Total
1	Norway	6	4	5	15
2	United States	2	2	2	6
3	Sweden	2	2	1	5
4	Finland	2	1	1	4
5 {	Canada	1	0	0	1
	France	1	0	0	1
6	Austria	0	3	1	4
7 {	Belgium	0	0	1	1
	Czechoslovakia	0	0	1	1
	Germany	0	0	1	1
	Great Britain	0	0	1	1
	Switzerland (host nation)	0	0	1	1

1928 Summer Olympics

Rank	Nation	Gold	Silver	Bronze	Total
1	United States	22	18	16	56
2	Germany	10	7	14	31
3	Finland	8	8	9	25
4	Sweden	7	6	12	25

5	Italy	7	5	7	19
6	Switzerland	7	4	4	15
7	France	6	10	5	21
8	Netherlands (host nation)	6	9	4	19
9	Hungary	4	5	0	9
10	Canada	4	4	7	15

1932 WINTER OLYMPICS

Rank	Nation	Gold	Silver	Bronze	Total
1	United States (host nation)	6	4	2	12
2	Norway	3	4	3	10
3	Canada	1	1	5	7
4	Sweden	1	2	0	3
5	Finland	1	1	1	3
6	Austria	1	1	0	2
7	France	1	0	0	1
8	Switzerland	0	1	0	1
9	Germany	0	0	2	2
10	Hungary	0	0	1	1

1932 SUMMER OLYMPICS

Rank	Nation	Gold	Silver	Bronze	Total
1	United States (host nation)	41	32	30	103
2	Italy	12	12	12	36
3	France	10	5	4	19
4	Sweden	9	5	9	23
5	Japan	7	7	4	18
6	Hungary	6	4	5	15
7	Finland	5	8	12	25
8	Great Britain	4	7	5	16
9	Germany	3	12	5	20
10	Australia	3	1	1	5

1936 Winter Olympics

Rank	Nation	Gold	Silver	Bronze	Total
1	Norway	7	5	3	15
2	Germany (host nation)	3	3	0	6
3	Sweden	2	2	3	7
4	Finland	1	2	3	6
5	Switzerland	1	2	0	3
6	Austria	1	1	2	4
7	Great Britain	1	1	1	3
8	United States	1	0	3	4
9	Canada	0	1	0	1
10 {	France	0	0	1	1
	Hungary	0	0	1	1

1936 Summer Olympics

Rank	Nation	Gold	Silver	Bronze	Total
1	Germany (host nation)	33	26	30	89
2	United States	24	20	12	56
3	Hungary	10	1	5	16
4	Italy	8	9	5	22
5 {	Finland	7	6	6	19
	France	7	6	6	19
6	Sweden	6	5	9	20
7	Japan	6	4	8	18
8	Netherlands	6	4	7	17
9	Great Britain	4	7	3	14

1948 Winter Olympics

Rank	Nation	Gold	Silver	Bronze	Total
1 {	Norway	4	3	3	10
	Sweden	4	3	3	10
2	Switzerland (host nation)	3	4	3	10
3	United States	3	4	2	9
4	France	2	1	2	5

5	Canada	2	0	1	3
6	Austria	1	3	4	8
7	Finland	1	3	2	6
8	Belgium	1	1	0	2
9	Italy	1	0	0	1

1948 SUMMER OLYMPICS

Rank	Nation	Gold	Silver	Bronze	Total
1	United States	38	27	19	84
2	Sweden	16	11	17	44
3	France	10	6	13	29
4	Hungary	10	5	12	27
5	Italy	8	11	8	27
6	Finland	8	7	5	20
7	Turkey	6	4	2	12
8	Czechoslovakia	6	2	3	11
9	Switzerland	5	10	5	20
10	Denmark	5	7	8	20

Notes

CHAPTER ONE

"Oh, I can't describe": Lucian, *Anacharsis*, quoted in Perrottet, *The Naked Olympics*, p. x.

"They evidently combined": Spivey, *The Ancient Olympics*, p. 112.

"from a fixed-feet position": Ibid., p. 92.

"At the sound of the bronze trumpet": Sophocles, *Electra*, pp. 165–167.

"Beauty in a young man": Aristotle, *The Basic Works of Aristotle*, p. 1341.

"They curled their whips": Homer, *The Iliad*, bk. 23, ll. 386–391.

"Let me tell you this": Ibid., ll. 672–676.

"They stepped into the middle": Ibid., ll. 686–689.

"with feet trailing": Ibid., ll. 696–698.

"where cunning intelligence counts": Spivey, *The Ancient Olympics*, p. 10.

"Now for the field and track": Homer, *The Odyssey*, bk. 8, ll. 97–103.

"Why do you young chaps": Ibid., ll. 154–158.

"You never learned a sport": Ibid., ll. 161–165.

"Odysseus frowned": Ibid., ll. 166–167.

"Anyone else?": Ibid., l. 208.

CHAPTER TWO

"There is no greater glory": Homer, *The Odyssey*, bk. 8, ll. 148–149.

"Not with money": Perrottet, *The Naked Olympics*, p. 85.

"Only those among you": Philostratus, *Life of Apollonius of Tyana*, 5.43.

"in short dresses unhitched at one shoulder": Spivey, *The Ancient Olympics*, p. 120.

"Aren't you scorched there": Epictetus, *Dissertations*, quoted in Swaddling, *The Ancient Olympic Games*, p. 7.

"People from all walks of life": Swaddling, *The Ancient Olympic Games*, p. 52.

"a calendar of competitive": Spivey, *The Ancient Olympics*, p. 70.

"Losers crept back to their mothers": Pindar, *Odes*, p. 183.

"because he never hurt anyone": Spivey, *The Ancient Olympics*, p. 166.

"took one look at his opponents": Ibid., p. 82.

"I was the invincible": Ibid., pp. 167–168.

"You say you want to be": Epictetus, quoted in Perrottet, *The Naked Olympics*, p. 47.

"hoisting a calf": Spivey, *The Ancient Olympics*, p. 63.

"threw it over his head with one hand": Ibid.

"float like a butterfly": http://quotations.about.com/od/stillmorefamouspeople/a/MuhammadAli1.htm.

"the biggest man of his times": Pausanias, quoted in Spivey, *The Ancient Olympics*, p. 108.

"came across a tree": Spivey, *The Ancient Olympics*, p. 101.

"to grab hold of," etc.: Ibid., pp. 17–18.

"I take no account of a man": Ibid., p. 25.

"cannot survive neediness": Ibid., p. 26.

"tripping one another up": Ibid., pp. 16–17.

"trained," "to fight the good fight," "athletes of Christ," etc.: Ibid., pp. 204–205.

"arrested": Tacitus, *The Annals of Imperial Rome*, p. 354.

Chapter Three

"when you have no other thing ado," "too obsessive a game": Haddon, *The First Ever English Olimpick Games*, p. 112.

"The important thing": Hill, *Olympic Politics*, p. 7.

"classic face," "brought me home": Poe, "To Helen," quoted in Williams, *An Anthology of American Verse*, p. 399.

"athletic chivalry": Coubertin, *The Olympic Idea*, p. 98.

"organized sport can create": Ibid., p. 13.

"the moral, physical": Wenlock Olympian Society Archives, www.wenlock-olympian-society.org.uk.

"The Olympic idea": Quoted in Spivey, *The Ancient Olympics,* p. 245.

Chapter Four

"absurd anachronism": Cropper, *Playing at Monarchy,* p. 172.

"modern": Ibid.

"To most Russians": Warner and Warner, *The Tide at Sunrise,* pp. 158–159.

"one Russian soldier was the equal": Ibid., p. 159.

Chapter Five

"This flag dips to no earthly King": www.bbc.co.uk/london /content/articles/2007/01/30/olympics_previous_london_feature .shtml.

"mathematical precision," "formal correctness": Guttmann, *The Olympics,* p. 32.

"Sir, you are the greatest athlete": MacLean, "Men You Wish You Were," www.primermagazine.com/2010/live/men-you-wish-you-were-jim-thorpe-worlds-greatest-athlete.

"Thanks, King": Ibid.

"was the greatest athlete": www.cmgww.com/sports/thorpe /quotes/quotes.html.

"Jim was very proud": Ibid.

"a magnificent performer": www.cmgww.com/sports/thorpe /bio/bio.html.

"In the name of all competitors": Wendl, "The Olympic Oath: A Brief History," p. 5.

"Citius, Altius, Fortius": Ibid.

"The most important thing": Ibid.

"Tarzan, Tarzan, welcome to Cuba!": www.tribuneindia.com /2000/20000917/spectrum/main7.htm.

"Nothing is more synonymous": Quoted in Kieran, Daley, and Jordan, *The Story of the Olympic Games,* p. 113.

CHAPTER SIX

"The sportive, knightly battle awakens": Chris Weigant, "The Olympic Torch Relay's Nazi Origin," *Huffington Post,* April 14, 2008, www.huffingtonpost.com/chris-weigant/the-olympic-torch-relays _b_96648.html.

"German sport has only one task": www.jewishvirtuallibrary .org/jsource/Holocaust/olympics.html.

"way to weed out the weak": Mandell, *The Nazi Olympics,* p. 50.

"white Jew": Guttmann, *The Games Must Go On,* p. 64.

"The very foundation": www.ushmm.org/museum/exhibit /online/olympics/detail.php?content-boycott.

"Jewish-Communist conspiracy": Mandell, *The Nazi Olympics,* p. 63.

"moral and financial": www.historyplace.com/worldwar2 /triumph/tr-olympics.htm.

"black victories would undermine": Perrottet, *The Naked Olympics,* p. 80.

"banned from city": www.historyplace.com/worldwar2 /triumph/tr-olympics.htm.

"laid out in the shape of": Perrottet, *The Naked Olympics,* p. 80.

"was the finest": www.historyplace.com/worldwar2/triumph /tr-olympics.htm.

"were ordered to refrain": Ibid.

"Greek 'high priestess' and fourteen": Perrottet, *The Naked Olympics,* p. 80.

"Buckeye Bullet": www.jesseowens.com.

"I let my feet spend as little time": Ibid.

"by having two Jews win gold": Halevi, "Games of Shame," p. 13.

"the Germans were saving": www.ushmm.org/museum /exhibit/online/olympics/detail.php?content-jewish_athletes_more +lang=en.

"Coach, you can't hide": Ibid.

"Coach, I've won my three": Ibid.

"You'll do as you're told": Ibid.

"If America didn't have": Povich, "Berlin, 1936."

"When I passed the chancellor": Owens, *The Jesse Owens Story*, p. 100.

"Hitler didn't snub me": Schaap, *Triumph*, p. 217.

"Each of the German victories": Speer, *Inside the Third Reich*, p. 73.

"It took a lot of courage": Schwartz, "Owens Pierced a Myth."

Picture Credits

Anastasios 71/Shutterstock: 51; Art Resource: cover, 8; Sergei Bachlakov/Shutterstock: 3; Ken Bate: 44–45; Eastimages/Shutterstock: 6; German Federal Archives: 92, 94, 100, 104, 107, 112, 115; Insuratelu Gabriela Gianina/Shutterstock: 21; Sadequl Hussain/Shutterstock: 18; David Iliff/Shutterstock: 73; IOC/Olympic Museum Collections: 76, 78 (bottom); Jayspy/Shutterstock: 83; Panos Karapanagiotis/Shutterstock: 22; Marshall Kramer: 74 (right); Library of Congress: 2, 46, 49 (top), 59, 60, 61 (top), 61 (bottom), 64, 65, 68, 69, 74 (left), 75, 79, 80, 81, (top), 81 (bottom), 82, 85, 87, 88, 102; Mike Liu/Shutterstock: 7; David Monniaux: 24; Marie-Lan Nguyen: 9, 10 (top), 13, 19, 37; Official Olympic Report: 77, 78 (top right); PD-Art: 12, 30, 31, 33, 34, 35, 44, 45 (top), 49 (bottom), 50 (top), 116; PD-US: 42, 50 (bottom), 52–53, 55, 56, 57, 58, 62, 63, 67, 70, 71, 72, 78 (top left), 116; Tatiana Popova/Shutterstock: 25, 27; Posztos/Shutterstock: 113; Leni Riefenstahl: 97, 98, 103, 109 (top), 109 (bottom), 110 (top), 110 (bottom); Wolfgang Sauber: 10 (bottom); Josef Jindřich Šechtl: 93; Zenodot Verlagsgesellschaft: 15.

Bibliography

Aristotle. *The Basic Works of Aristotle.* Edited by Richard McKeon. New York: Random House, 1941.

Baker, William J. *Jesse Owens: An American Life.* New York: Free Press, 1986.

Bernotas, Bob. *Jim Thorpe: Sac and Fox Athlete.* New York: Chelsea House, 1992.

Coubertin, Pierre de. *The Olympic Idea: Discourses and Essays.* Lausanne: Editions Internationales Olympiques, 1970.

Cropper, Corry. *Playing at Monarchy: Sport as Metaphor in Nineteenth-Century France.* Lincoln: University of Nebraska Press, 2008.

Drees, L. *Olympia: Gods, Artists and Athletes.* London: Pall Mall Press, 1968.

Finding, John E., and Kimberly D. Pelle. *Historical Dictionary of the Modern Olympic Movement.* Westport, Conn.: Greenwood, 1996.

Finley, M. I., and H. W. Pleket. *The Olympic Games: The First Thousand Years.* London: Chatto and Windus, 1976.

Gardiner, E. Norman. *Athletics of the Ancient World.* London: Ares, 1930.

Golden, Mark. *Sport and Society in Ancient Greece.* Cambridge: Cambridge University Press, 1998.

———. *Sport in the Ancient World from A to Z.* London: Routledge, 2004.

Greenberg, Stan. *The Guinness Book of Olympics: Facts and Feats.* London: Guinness, 1996.

Guttmann, Allen. *From Ritual to Record: The Nature of Modern Sports.* New York: Columbia University Press, 1978.

———. *The Games Must Go On: Avery Brundage and the Olympic Movement.* New York: Columbia University Press, 1984.

———. *The Olympics: A History of the Modern Games.* Urbana: University of Illinois Press, 1992.

Haddon, Celia. *The First Ever English Olimpick Games.* London: Hodder and Stoughton, 2004.

Halevi, Charles Chi. "Games of Shame." *Jerusalem Post,* April 10, 2000.

Harris, H. A. *Greek Athletes and Athletics.* Bloomington: University of Indiana Press, 1966.

———. *Sport in Greece and Rome.* London: Thames and Hudson, 1972.

Hart-Davis, Duff. *Hitler's Games: The 1936 Olympics.* London: Century Hutchinson, 1986.

Hill, Christopher R. *Olympic Politics.* Manchester: Manchester University Press, 1996.

Hillenbrand, Laura. *Unbroken: A World War II Story of Survival, Resilience, and Redemption.* New York: Random House, 2010.

www.history.com

Homer. *The Iliad.* Translated by Stanley Lombardo. Indianapolis: Hackett, 1997.

———. *The Odyssey.* Translated by Robert Fitzgerald. New York: Doubleday Anchor, 1963.

"International Olympic Games in Athens, 1906." *Journal of Olympic History* 10 (2001): 10–27.

Josephson, Judith Pinkerton. *Jesse Owens, Track and Field Legend.* Springfield, N.J.: Enslow, 1997.

Kieran, John, Arthur Daley, and Pat Jordan. *The Story of the Olympic Games, 776 B.C. to 1976.* Philadelphia: J. B. Lippincott, 1969.

Kyle, D. G. *Athletics in Ancient Athens.* Leiden: E. J. Brill, 1987.

Lee, Hugh M. *Nikephoros Beihefte: The Program and Schedule of the Ancient Olympic Games.* Hildesheim: Weidmann, 2002.

MacAloon, John J. *This Great Symbol: Pierre de Coubertin and the Origins of the Modern Olympic Games.* Chicago: University of Chicago Press, 1981.

MacLean, Kevin H. "Men You Wish You Were: Jim Thorpe, World's Greatest Athlete." *Primer.* www.primermagazine.com/2010/live /men-you-wish-you-were-jim-thorpe-worlds-greatest-athlete.

Mandell, Richard D. *The Nazi Olympics.* New York: Macmillan, 1971.

Margolick, David. "Zamperini's War." *New York Times Book Review,* November 21, 2010.

Miller, Stephen G. *Ancient Greek Athletics.* New Haven, Conn.: Yale University Press, 2004.

———, ed. *Arete: Greek Sports from Ancient Sources.* Berkeley: University of California Press, 1991.

Newby, Z. *Greek Athletics in the Roman World: Victory and Virtue.* Oxford: Oxford University Press, 2005.

Nish, Ian. *The Origins of the Russo-Japanese War.* New York: Longman, 1985.

Nuwer, Hank. *The Legend of Jesse Owens.* New York: F. Watts, 1998.

Owens, Jesse. *Blackthink: My Life as Black Man and White Man.* New York: William Morrow, 1970.

———. *The Jesse Owens Story.* New York: G. P. Putnam's Sons, 1971.

Pausanias. *Guide to Greece.* Edited by Peter Levi. 2 vols. New York: Penguin Books, 1971.

www.pbs.org

Perrottet, Tony. *The Naked Olympics: The True Story of the Ancient Games.* New York: Random House, 2004.

Philostratus, Flavius. *Life of Apollonius of Tyana.* Translated by F. C. Conybeare. 2 vols. Loeb Classical Library. Cambridge, Mass.: Harvard University Press, 2005.

Pindar. *Odes.* Loeb Classical Library. Cambridge, Mass.: Harvard University Press, 1970.

Plato. *Collected Dialogues.* Edited by Edith Hamilton and Huntington Cairns. Princeton, N.J.: Princeton University Press, 1971.

Poliakoff, Michael. *Combat Sports in the Ancient World: Competition, Violence, and Culture.* New Haven, Conn.: Yale University Press, 1987.

Povich, Shirley. "Berlin, 1936: At the Olympics, Achievements of the Brave in a Year of Cowardice." *Washington Post,* July 6, 1996.

Raschke, Wendy J., ed. *The Archaeology of the Olympics: The Olympics and Other Festivals in Antiquity.* Madison: University of Wisconsin Press, 1988.

Sansone, D. *Greek Athletics and the Genesis of Sport.* Berkeley: University of California Press, 1988.

Scanlon, Thomas F. *Eros and Greek Athletics.* Oxford: Oxford University Press, 2002.

———. *Greek and Roman Athletics: A Bibliography.* Chicago: Ares, 1984.

———. *Olympia and Macedonia: Games, Gymnasia, and Politics.* Toronto: Thessalonikeans Society of Metro Toronto, 1997.

Schaap, Jeremy. *Triumph: The Untold Story of Jesse Owens and Hitler's Olympics.* New York: Houghton Mifflin Harcourt, 2007.

Schwartz, Larry. "Owens Pierced a Myth." ESPN.com. http://espn.go.com/sportscentury/features/00016393.html.

Segrave, Jeffrey O. *The Olympic Games in Transition.* Champaign: University of Illinois Press, 1986.

Sinn, Ulrich. *Olympia: Cult, Sport, and Ancient Festival.* Princeton, N.J.: Markus Weiner, 2000.

Sophocles. *Electra.* In *The Complete Greek Tragedies,* ed. David Grene and Richmond Lattimore. Vol. 4. New York: Modern Library, 1957.

Speer, Albert. *Inside the Third Reich.* London: Macmillan, 1970.

Spivey, Nigel. *The Ancient Olympics.* Oxford: Oxford University Press, 2004.

Swaddling, Judith. *The Ancient Olympic Games.* Austin: University of Texas Press, 2008.

Sweet, Waldo E. *Sport and Recreation in Ancient Greece.* Oxford: Oxford University Press, 1987.

Tacitus. *The Annals of Imperial Rome.* Translated by Michael Grant. New York: Penguin Books, 1966.

Tibballs, Geoff. *The Olympics' Strangest Moments.* London: Robson Books, 2004.

Tupper, Harmon. *To the Great Ocean: Siberia and the Trans-Siberian Railway.* London: Secker and Warburg, 1965.

Valavanis, P. *Games and Sanctuaries in Ancient Greece: Olympia, Delphi, Isthmia, Nemea, Athens.* Los Angeles: Getty Publications, 2004.

Walder, David. *The Short Victorious War: The Russo-Japanese Conflict 1904–5.* New York: Harper and Row, 1973.

Warner, Denis, and Peggy Warner. *The Tide at Sunrise: A History of the Russo-Japanese War, 1904–1905.* Portland, Ore.: Frank Cass Publishers, 1974.

Wendl, Karel. "The Olympic Oath: A Brief History." *Journal of Olympic History,* Winter 1995, pp. 4–5.

Wenlock Olympian Society Archives. www.wenlock-olympian -society.org.uk.

Williams, Oscar, ed. *An Anthology of American Verse.* New York: World Publishing, 1966.

Young, David C. *A Brief History of the Olympic Games.* Oxford: Blackwell Publishing, 2004.

———. *The Modern Olympics: A Struggle for Revival.* Baltimore: Johns Hopkins University Press, 1996.

———. *The Olympic Myth of Greek Amateur Athletics.* Chicago: Ares, 1985.

Index

Note: *Italic* page numbers refer to illustrations.

Acknowledgments

Life is short, art long—even when a book is not, comparatively speaking.

So it always gives me great pleasure to acknowledge those who helped along the way. Many friends took delight in this project, as did my family, with their sideline cheers. But I owe a more obvious and specific debt to those who have written before me on the history of the Games. The excellent and reliable works of David C. Young, M. I. Finley, John Kieran, Arthur Daley, Pat Jordan, Thomas F. Scanlon, Nigel Spivey, Tony Perrottet, Judith Swaddling, and Allen Guttmann deserve to be singled out, along with numerous other books, articles, and websites that enabled me to imagine the proper story and fill in the details.

The staff at Knopf could not have been more helpful. I am immensely grateful to the care and consideration of my magnificent editor, Michelle Frey, who gave me every leeway to get things right. In this, she worked closely with her very able assistant, Kelly Delaney, who did a spectacular job with the picture research and handled numerous details with spirit and skill. The splendid book and jacket design was developed by Kate Gartner; the copyediting department, with particular thanks to Artie Bennett, Jennifer Healey, and Amy Schroeder, saved me from some significant oversights and errors and was nothing if not thorough and exacting.

By all of the above (in a punning analogy to volleyball), the book was well served. With her well-sneakered bounce and support, my wife, Hilary, helped get the ball over the net.